WELL
SPOKEN

WELL SPOKEN

SPOKEN

TEACHING SPEAKING TO ALL STUDENTS

ERIK PALMER

FOREWORD BY KELLY GALLAGHER

STENHOUSE PUBLISHERS
PORTLAND, MAINE

Stenhouse Publishers
www.stenhouse.com

Library of Congress Cataloging-in-Publication Data
Palmer, Erik, 1953–
    Well spoken : teaching speaking to all students / Erik Palmer.
        p. cm.
    Includes bibliographical references.
    ISBN 978-1-57110-881-4 (pbk. : alk. paper) -- ISBN 978-1-57110-907-1 (e-book)
    1. Public speaking. I. Title.
    PN4129.15.P35 2011
    808.5' 1071 -- dc22

                             2010050307

Cover and interior design by Blue Design (www.bluedes.com)

Manufactured in the United States of America

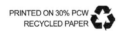
PRINTED ON 30% PCW
RECYCLED PAPER

17 16 15 14 13 12 11 9 8 7 6 5 4 3 2 1

CONTENTS

FOREWORD

By Kelly Gallagher

I n this Age of Testing, there is often a disconnect between what students need to learn and what students are actually being taught. Multiple-choice assessments have driven deeper reading out of our classrooms, and writing has been pushed to the back burner. But of all the language arts, there is one that has been especially shortchanged by this blind adherence to state testing: the art of speaking. This vital life skill has been all but ignored in many classrooms simply because the ability to give an effective speech is not tested on most state assessments.

Veering away from teaching students how to speak effectively does not bode well for our children. Students sitting in our classrooms today will soon enter a world where virtually every business survey emphasizes the importance of verbal communication skills—a world where one's ability to present, perform, and persuade will prove more important than ever. Clearly, for the next generation of students, speaking well is a foundational skill.

In *Well Spoken*, Erik Palmer recognizes and addresses the fundamental difference between talking and speaking. All of our students know how to talk; unfortunately, very few of them know how to speak. If our students are going to become effective speakers, they need us—their teachers—to teach them the art of speech. This is where *Well Spoken* excels. Clearly written and full of numerous effective strategies, *Well Spoken* offers invaluable advice and tools for teachers who recognize the importance of teaching the art of speech.

Palmer's approach to teaching speech mirrors what we know about effective teaching of the writing process. He begins by teaching his students the importance of understanding purpose and audience and how these two elements play an integral part in crafting a speech. In subsequent chapters Palmer offers numerous helpful tips, including how to start speeches with "attention-holding elements" (hooks), how to help a student organize a speech into a coherent sequence, how to craft effective transitions, and how to leave listeners with a powerful conclusion.

Well Spoken is more than a guide for helping students write better speeches. It also contains many practical ideas for teaching students how to *deliver* better speeches. As Palmer notes, "How a speech is performed may be more important than how it is built." With this in mind, *Well Spoken* offers excellent strategies to help students be poised, to capture the right tone and voice, to achieve the right kind of eye contact, and to be aware of how one's appearance and actions affect a speech.

After reading *Well Spoken*, I am motivated to give the teaching of speech a more prominent place in my classroom. I am especially grateful for Palmer's insightful work and his concrete steps to help me become a better speech teacher. If, like me, you are striving to prepare your students for the demands of the real world, I'm certain you will recognize the significance and value of Palmer's ideas and strategies, and will be energized to include them in your teaching repertoire.

ACKNOWLEDGMENTS

How did I get here? I don't ask myself that often, though it seems that I often end up someplace quite different than originally planned. When I asked the question, "How did I end up writing a book?" it led me to the realization that I needed to acknowledge many people who led me to this point.

I taught with Judi Herm. Her sons went to a different school, and when she saw how I taught speaking skills she wanted her sons to get that instruction. She contacted the school and suggested they hire me. They did, year after year. Thanks, Judi, for leading me to expand my audience and for opening many other doors.

Midge Kral worked at the school Judi sent me to. Midge could not have been a more enthusiastic fan and supporter. When she left that school, she began working at a bookstore and connected me with the store's owner. Thanks, Midge, for your wonderful support and spirit, as well as for the connection.

Sue Lubeck owns the bookstore. The Bookies is a warm, inviting place full of book lovers and helpful employees. Sue saw the first version of this book and thought it had promise, so she contacted Philippa Stratton at Stenhouse Publishers and put in a good word for me. Apparently, if Sue talks, people listen. Thanks, Sue, for promoting my ideas to Stenhouse, for running a fine independent bookstore, and for hosting my first book signing.

Philippa Stratton called me and asked for copies of my writing, which she sent to various readers for input. Thanks, Philippa, for believing in the book and advancing it.

Holly Holland at Stenhouse was one of those readers. She gave me detailed feedback on the book and a very positive response. She was instrumental in persuading Stenhouse to publish it. As my editor, Holly offered consistently brilliant advice. I always thought, "Yeah, that *is* better" when I read her suggestions. Thanks, Holly, for helping the book along and for improving my writing.

Kelley Gaskill worked for Academy School District 20 in Colorado

Springs. She came to a presentation I did for the Colorado Language Arts Society and said, "Can you come train the teachers in my district?" Kelley was the first to think of implementing the ideas district-wide, years before oral communication was added to the state standards. At one of the workshops, a participant asked, "Why isn't there a book on this for general classroom teachers?" which gave me the idea to write one. Thanks, Kelley, for your foresight, your support, and your positive comments about my work.

Debra Fine is a successful author and the mother of two former students of mine. She always says great things about her children's experiences in my class. She also taught me how to go through the process of writing and publishing a book. Thanks, Debra, for your positive thoughts and for your mentoring.

I have to acknowledge my sons, Greg and Ross. They were the test cases. They took the lessons I taught them and proved beyond any doubt that my approach to teaching speaking works. In many realms—theatrical performance, speech contest, interview, corporate event management, wedding officiant, social occasion—they have had enormous success. I could not be more proud of them.

And what is it worth to have someone who totally believes in you? Many times have I heard, "You *should* do that. You would be great at it!" when I thought of moving into a new venture. My wife, Anne, has always been encouraging and uplifting. She is a powerful person and that power inspires me. Thank you, Anne.

PART I
THE ART OF PUBLIC SPEAKING

Speaking well really is an art, though most of us have been speaking since we were young children. Carefully choosing our words, organizing our ideas so they are easy to follow, captivating an audience by employing effective gestures, or pacing our speech for emphasis—these are the building blocks of good public speaking. Every student can learn them, practice them, and perform them. But first, they need conscientious teachers who will show them how.

That's where you come in.

CHAPTER 1:

Can We Talk?

W hat percentage of communication is oral and what percentage is written?

Think about your typical day. Start at your home. How often do you communicate with people around you in writing? As a parent, are you handing notes to your children? E-mailing them? Texting them? Occasionally, perhaps, but overwhelmingly you are talking to them. Are you using paper and pencil to communicate with your spouse or roommate? Maybe you leave a note on the counter as a reminder to take out the garbage, but when the discussion shifts to whose turn it is and who took it out last week, you talk.

And when you get to school, how do you interact with coworkers and teammates? Yes, you can iChat them with a quick question, but the vast majority of your interaction is verbal. You tell stories about what happened of interest in your classroom today, you discuss team plans for the future, and you ask your colleagues about their home lives. How do you interact with the principal? If you write an e-mail to an administrator, isn't it often a request for a face-to-face meeting? And what about your students' families? They want to talk to you. Send a note sometime and suggest that you don't need to meet them and would rather handle things with e-mail. Imagine the response. Your students' parents want to hear your voice.

Step back in time. How did you select your mate? After many long conversations, right? How did you get your job? A résumé might have gotten you in the door, but an interview most likely got you the job. Your ability to speak well (or at least better than the other people applying) was crucial to getting hired. How many other significant events in your life can you think of in which your ability to speak well mattered? A wedding toast? A eulogy? Inspiring the tee ball team you got conned into coaching? If these events haven't occurred yet in your life, they will. There are many, many opportunities for meaningful speeches in a normal life. Simply put, oral communication is our predominant way of communicating.

LET'S STOP SQUEEZING OUT PUBLIC SPEAKING

Now, let me make a radical statement: the mission of education should not be to make students better at school but rather to prepare them for life. As schools focus on high-stakes testing, there is a tendency to forget that mission and to see the test as the ultimate outcome of our instruction. As a result, many important parts of a well-rounded education that do not directly contribute to the test score can end up on the cutting room floor, including art, music, physical education, home economics, health, and civics. Another skill commonly sacrificed is speaking.

There is some evidence that the atmosphere is changing. Colorado, my home state, revised its state standards in 2010. The 1995 standard "Reading and Writing" became "Reading, Writing, and Communicating," and "Oral Expression" is the first thing mentioned under the standard. The Common Core State Standards Initiative suggests adopting the standard "Speaking and Listening." More than forty states had adopted the Common Core Standards by the end of 2010. Some school districts have added formal speaking assessments to the curriculum, though such districts are still the exception, not the rule. I believe that, to a large extent, these changes are driven by a new concern for workplace readiness and a desire to think beyond the classroom and beyond the high-stakes test.

While speaking skills may have been somewhat underemphasized in schools, they have not been underemphasized in the real world. Look at the business section of your local bookstore. There are many, many books on the shelves about public speaking. Some focus on general presentation skills, some on specific skills like closing the deal, some on overcoming fear, and some on speaking in social settings. All of them recognize the importance of being well spoken.

Speaking well enables us to communicate clearly with coworkers and avoid misunderstandings on the job. Speaking well enables us to feel more confident and become more respectable. (I recall a conversation with our school psychologist, who told me that she felt my opinions had more power than those of my colleagues because I spoke so well. She didn't say my opinions *were* better. They just *seemed* better, which I suppose is still a compliment.) Speaking well enables us to be more impressive over the telephone and in video conferences. Speaking well is crucial to professional promotion. No CEO of a corporation can lead without strong oral communication. No attorney can persuade a jury, no politician can be elected, and no coach can motivate a team without strong speaking skills. Even in professions that we don't think of as highly verbal, oral communication matters. Wouldn't you prefer to do business with an electrician who speaks well? A landscaper? A hairdresser?

Why not make clear to students how important speaking is to professional success? Students often believe that what we teach in school has no relevance to their lives in the "real world," and to a large extent, they may be right. I'm willing to bet that people who speak well have more professional and social success in life than people who don't. That's relevance.

Every year, the National Association of Colleges and Employers (NACE) surveys employers to see what qualities they want most from college students they are considering for employment. Employers responding to NACE's *Job Outlook 2011* survey suggest that "New college graduates looking to crack the still-tight job market need to hone their verbal communication skills . . . verbal communication skills topped the list of 'soft' skills they seek in new college graduates looking to join their organizations" (National Association of Colleges and Employers 2010). Strong work ethic, teamwork skills, analytical skills, and initiative, while all critical skills, followed verbal communication in importance. If students master speaking, their chances of success increase dramatically.

Further support for the value of speaking skills comes from a study of 104 Silicon Valley employers. Silicon Valley is the home of many of America's high-tech firms, and you might expect that they would place a high value on math and engineering skills, right? Company representatives were asked several questions about desired qualities in prospective employees. The question "What additional business communication skills would you like to see in your recent college graduate new hires?" produced interesting results:

> *Employers sought improved oral presentation skills more frequently than they did written skills.* Their comments expressed *a need for stronger skills in public speaking*, enhanced interpersonal skills, increased confidence, and improved interviewing skills. Several wrote that students needed *more presentation skills*, highlighting the ability to use software tools like PowerPoint. This was surprising, because the popular press talks more about a lack of writing skills among college graduates than about insufficient oral skills. (Stevens 2005, 7; emphasis added)

On a personal note, my former student Kelly affirmed my belief in the value of teaching speaking. She looked me up twenty-one years after being in my middle school English class. She wanted to tell me about her marriage and her master's degree, and she wanted to let me know that I had influenced her more than any other teacher. Kelly took me out to dinner and told me that she believed that what I taught her in my English class was more responsible for her success than anything else she had learned. Of course, I was curious. Was it alliteration? The plot line diagram? Identifying main characters? Writing topic sentences? No, Kelly said the most vital skill she had learned from me was how to speak well and be comfortable in front of people. Let me be clear: I am not saying that we should forget about all those other critical language skills. But while those are all essential, Kelly picked speaking skills as the *most* important.

"LIKE, WE KNOW THEY CAN, LIKE, TALK, BUT HOW DO I TEACH THEM TO SPEAK?"

Consider that teachers spend untold hours showing students how to communicate through writing. We have specific lessons about commas, capitalization, word choice, topic sentences, and so on, as we should.

But public speaking? Well, we might have one required speech during the year that we grade based on a rubric that mentions eye contact. In my experience, however, very few teachers specifically teach the skills needed to make that speech more successful. *After* the speech, we might give some comments as feedback, but that's about it, right? Where are the specific lessons about hand gestures, analyzing the audience, or using pacing for emphasis?

All students can talk (sometimes we need to ask them to stop!) and, therefore, teachers often assume they don't need to offer instruction in verbal communication. But listen to what they say: "I'm all like, whoa, what is that about, but he is like, whatever, I don't know what you mean, so I like get all mad and ready to, like, leave but suddenly he, like, changes, know what I mean?"

Are you impressed? Could your students benefit from some more instruction?

Imagine walking into a ninth-grade English class to observe the teacher. As you enter, the teacher informs you that he will not be teaching writing this year because the students already know how to write. The teacher can prove this and shows you the "What I did this summer" paragraphs, text messages, and entries from online chat rooms. That seems absurd, doesn't it? It is equally absurd when you imagine the teacher saying this about speaking: "I will not be teaching speaking this year because my students already know how to speak." Students need direct instruction to help them speak effectively, just as they need direct instruction to learn how to write effectively.

THE PARTS OF A SPEECH

Perhaps I have persuaded you that developing effective speaking skills is worth more time than it usually receives in classrooms, but there is still the issue of how to teach speaking. That is where this book comes in. Effective speaking involves specific skills. This book explains those skills and how to teach them. I have not written a workbook full of handouts to give to students. Books like that already exist, and to find them you may want to check the teacher's helper store in your community. Such workbooks leave something to be desired, however. Yes, they include speaking activities and attractive reproducible worksheets, but they offer little or no direction about how to prepare students to perform the activities. This book provides a framework for teaching speaking and ensuring that students understand what the workbooks are talking about.

I developed the ideas in this book during twenty-one years as a classroom teacher—primarily as an English teacher, but I also taught math, science, and civics—and during ten years as an educational consultant. I have worked directly with thousands of students and have taught hundreds of teachers how to teach speaking skills to students.

But education was my second career. I started in the business world as the manager of a commodity brokerage firm, and oral communication was a crucial part of the job. My speaking ability helped me become the national sales leader for my firm. When I moved to the classroom, I incorporated speaking activities in all the subjects I taught. I discovered that the skills described by the acronym PVLEGS (poise, voice, life, eye contact, gestures, and speed), which I discuss in Part III, provided students of all ages with a simple way to grasp the elements of effective speaking. In addition, middle and high school students gained the confidence and skills to be highly successful in speaking contests sponsored by groups such as the Optimist Club and DECA (Distributive Education Clubs of America). And of course, like Kelly, former students would mention that the concepts worked in later life, too.

My hope is that this book will be useful for all teachers, from elementary grades through high school. The examples tend to be from the middle school level for two reasons: that is where most of my personal teaching experience occurred, and middle school level concepts and activities can usually be modified to suit other levels. After reading in Chapter 5 about the organization component of building a speech, the second-grade teacher may decide to ignore the transitions part and focus on having students grasp the need for an introduction, body, and conclusion (a beginning, middle, and end in second-grade language). The high school teacher may gloss over the basic format of a speech and teach a lesson about using sophisticated transitions. After reading in Chapter 13 about the speed component of performing a speech, the elementary teacher may focus only on the need to avoid speaking too fast, whereas the high school teacher can work on developing dramatic pauses.

The book is also intended to be useful for those who work with students in after-school clubs. DECA, FBLA (Future Business Leaders of America), Robotics, Odyssey of the Mind, and more all have opportunities for students to showcase oral skills. In many competitions, judges base their decision on who has the better presentation, not on who has the better product.

YOU CAN DO THIS!

Have you ever been amazed that, after something was pointed out to you, you hadn't thought of it before? There may be moments like that as you read this book. "Of course! Why didn't I teach them that?" There will be some speaking components that you knew in the back of your mind but never consciously thought about and some speaking skills that you assumed everyone already knew. What I hope to do is make the art of speaking understandable and make your teaching of speaking purposeful.

Let me emphasize two important points. First, when I mention public speaking throughout the book, I am not referring only to a formal presentation in front of a large audience. Public speaking encompasses a wide variety of genres, from interviews, discussions, debates, toasts, stage presentations, answering questions in class, negotiating business deals, all the way up to standing on the steps of the Lincoln Memorial in front of half a million people. In other words, I am referring to all the forms of speaking beyond casual banter with friends. Elements of public speaking are involved in all of those situations.

Second, you don't have to be a master orator to teach speaking. You simply have to understand how master orators create their magic, and you have to be willing to commit to improving the oral communication skills of your students. But you may find after reading this book that *you* have become a better speaker, too, and back-to-school night will never frighten or intimidate you again.

CHAPTER 2:

Effective Communication

Take a look at the following two essays.

SAMPLE ESSAY 1

The war in Iraq was a good idea. Saddam Hussein was a bad man. He did bad things to people in his country. He said he wanted to attack America and send terrorists to attack us. That might have killed a lot of Americans. The United States is for freedom. We should give freedom to Iraq. For these reasons, we should attack Iraq.

SAMPLE ESSAY 2

the situation in iraq is extremely complex. wile it is true that Husein is a ruthless dictater he was holding together a country that has sevral waring factions for 1300 years shiites and sunis have been in a religus war and the ethnic kurds have been battling iraquis, without a strong man the country would brake into a civil war. Looking at what mite have hapened without him, he may actully have been good for iraq When the united States attacked the balence was iretrivably upset and we may have caused problems that cant be solved.

What grade would you give each essay? Essay 1 is perfectly capital-ized, perfectly spelled, perfectly punctuated. Should Essay 1 receive an A grade? Essay 2 is full of problems with capitalization, spelling, and punctuation. Should that paper get an F? Most of us would have a hard time accepting those grades. Essay 1 indicates very little understand-ing of the problems involved in the Iraq War debate. Does that mean it deserves an F? Essay 2 demonstrates an understanding of the problem, but does it deserve an A? Again, most of us would say no.

Years ago, teachers were making decisions exactly like this. They assessed a piece of writing with only one grade. Maybe both essays would get a C, albeit for very different reasons. At some point, teach-ers realized that writing is a collection of various parts, which means that a single grade is not always useful. Rather, we must examine the parts. Content, word choice, sentence structure, writing conventions, paragraphing, organization, and perhaps other traits must be analyzed separately.

Look back at the two essays. If we graded each essay based on two aspects of writing, Essay 1 would get top marks for writing conventions but low marks for content. Essay 2 would get the reverse. The grades entered in the grade book might end up being the same, but if the teacher explained how the two aspects of writing were assessed, the students would have an understanding of what the grades represented. With specific writing traits delineated, the authors can focus on areas of strength and weakness.

A multiple-trait framework was a great advancement in writing instruction. Effective speaking is also a collection of various parts, so let me suggest, then, a multiple-trait framework for speaking. A new way of looking at oral communication will make it easier to teach the skills involved and will make it easier for students to become competent communicators.

In Figure 2.1, you will see a rubric currently used by a prominent school district near my home.

FIGURE 2.1: GENERIC RUBRIC FOR SPEAKING ACTIVITIES

ADVANCED

- The student delivers the speech effectively to inform, explain, demonstrate, or persuade.
- The student organizes the formal speech using an introduction, body, and conclusion with transitions and well-integrated evidence.
- Subject, vocabulary, and delivery are adapted effectively to the audience and the occasion.

PROFICIENT

- The student delivers the speech appropriately to inform, explain, demonstrate, or persuade.
- The student organizes the formal speech using an introduction, body, and conclusion with transitions and evidence.
- Subject, vocabulary, and delivery are adapted appropriately to the audience and the occasion.

BASIC

- The student delivers the speech to inform, explain, demonstrate, or persuade.
- The student organizes the formal speech using a beginning, middle, and end.
- The student's vocabulary and delivery convey the message.

PRE-BASIC

- The student attempts to inform, explain, demonstrate, or persuade through a formal speech.
- Organization of the speech lacks a beginning, middle, and/or end.

I will comment much more extensively on rubrics in Chapter 15. Here I want to focus on the elements of effective speaking. According to the rubric in Figure 2.1, an advanced speaker "effectively" delivers the speech, but a proficient speaker "appropriately" delivers the speech. Is this a useful distinction? I am not sure that a student would know what distinguishes *effective* subject, vocabulary, and delivery from *appropriate* subject, vocabulary, and delivery. The advanced speech has "well-integrated evidence," but the proficient only has "evidence." Again, I am not sure a student will understand the difference. Unfortunately, we often give rubrics to our students with descriptors that make no sense to them.

Focusing more specifically on our purpose in this book, this rubric doesn't accurately reflect the components of a good speech. Subject, vocabulary, and delivery are lumped together in one bullet point. Those are radically different things. Think back to the sample essays about Iraq and imagine grading them using a rubric bullet point that includes "content and punctuation are appropriate for the purpose." It seems absurd now, in the multiple-trait writing world, to put those together, and it is equally absurd to group subject, vocabulary, and delivery in a rubric meant to evaluate speaking skills. Delivery alone has several components. The solution is to break the art of speaking into meaningful pieces and to develop a multiple-trait framework for oral communication.

Public speaking can be divided into two distinct categories: building a speech and performing a speech. Both parts are crucial to understanding effective speech, yet teachers often miss the distinction. Most of us realize that presidents have speechwriters. Most of us know there are screenwriters and playwrights who compose the lines actors deliver. Most of us realize that some person has written the news that the newscaster reads off the teleprompter. Obviously, these written words are only the beginning. After that, someone must perform the speech, deliver the lines, or read aloud the news. The performing talent is very different than the writing talent. The person who builds the speech for the president or the newscaster might have a very difficult time performing the speech himself or herself. Conversely, though the newscaster might look good and sound good, he or she may be a terrible writer, just as the actor who can beautifully deliver the lines may have no ability to write a script.

We may have realized intuitively that these two parts of speaking are distinct, but we may not have paid close attention to the distinction. Look back at the speaking rubric in Figure 2.1. Does the rubric indicate an understanding of the two main components of public speaking, building a speech and performing it? Unfortunately, no. Our first job is to clarify the difference between building a speech and performing a speech.

You will have students who are great at building a speech and dreadful at performing it. You will have students who are masterful performers but have nothing of value to say. These situations should come as no surprise. They are no different than having a student who can spell perfectly but who shows weak word choice, or having a student with sophisticated content in his or her writing but a limited ability to spell. We won't succeed at teaching students well until we can be specific about which skills need to be improved.

PART II
BUILDING A SPEECH

Before I open my mouth to speak, there are several things I need to do. I refer to these preparatory tasks as the "building a speech" stage. Obviously, I must have something to say. If I want my comments to be worth listening to, I have to choose the most effective words. But because speakers are also seen, building a good speech involves more than just assembling words. I break the process into five parts:

> Audience: Understanding the Listeners
> Content: Making the Message Valuable
> Organization: Making the Speech Easy to Follow
> Visual Aids: Enhancing the Words
> Appearance: Dressing for the Occasion

Each of these parts is important. It may seem daunting to have five new skills to teach, but some of the elements overlap with the elements of building an effective piece of writing. And for those of you who are worried about the state assessment, this is the first of many times that I will point out: *Teaching speaking reinforces teaching writing*.

CHAPTER 3:

Audience: Understanding the Listeners

D o you speak the same way in your classroom as you do in the teachers' lounge? You probably would not still have your job if you did. If you were asked to give a five-minute speech on student behavior, wouldn't your first question be, "For whom?" For new teachers? For the PTO? For students in your class? For the comedy club? It makes a difference. At some level, we all know that speech must be adjusted to suit the situation.

Students do not have a hard time grasping this concept. Your students will readily admit that the language they use with Grandma is different from the language they use with their friends. Most are sophisticated enough to know that you "work" Dad differently than you "work" Mom. Intuitively, they understand that the audience we are addressing affects our speech. Therefore, the first part of building a speech involves purposefully analyzing the audience.

Consider the questions in Figure 3.1.

FIGURE 3.1: KNOW YOUR AUDIENCE BEFORE YOU SPEAK
Professional speakers typically ask these questions before they speak:

What is the average age of the audience members?
What is the age range?
What percentage is male and what percentage is female?
What is the educational level of the audience?
What does the audience already know about the topic?

What does the audience want from the speech?
What are the interests of the audience?
What are the biases of the audience?

Let me interject a short story. I was asked to give an after-dinner speech to students who had just completed their apprenticeships and were becoming journeymen electricians. I was quite good at preparing to speak to eighth-grade students in class, parents at school functions, and teachers at inservice trainings, but journeymen electricians? I sent the set of questions in Figure 3.1 to the director of the school and found out that the average age of the audience members was about thirty-five, but the age range was twenty-five to forty. That made it clear to me that I should not refer to things that baby boomers would know about the 1960s, nor should I refer to current teen pop culture. The audience was 60 percent male and 40 percent female, so I couldn't use only sports metaphors and locker room stories. The audience members had high school diplomas but not college degrees, and most had completed four years of electrical instruction. Knowing this, I could adjust my vocabulary as well as research something about electricians so I could speak more knowledgeably about their field.

It was crucial to know what the audience wanted from my speech. Was I supposed to merely entertain? Was I supposed to offer congratulations? Advice? Finally, I found out from the "interests" question that these were all union members. Most had young children, and many loved tinkering with and talking about cars. I'm sure you can see how that information would help me craft a speech specifically for this audience. You build a very different speech about electricity if your audience is a class of fourth graders than you do for graduates of the Electrical Apprenticeship and Training Committee. I never think of making a presentation as a professional speaker without collecting the answers to those questions about the audience.

Such questions don't just apply to after-dinner speeches. It is important to let students know that to connect with any audience, even an audience of only one person, they must understand the members' backgrounds. Teach students that analyzing the audience is a lifelong skill. Before a job interview, they will want to know something about the people they will encounter in the interview and the products the company makes. Before a sales presentation, they will want to have a customer profile to discover what the customer needs or wants. Before they meet their future in-laws, they will want to prepare by asking their fiancé good background questions in order to avoid the fate of any previous suitors.

Analyzing the audience is valuable in classroom settings as well. The simplest question is, *Who is the audience for the speech?* Invariably, students giving a speech look primarily at the teacher. Most likely, students were never instructed about the audience they are supposed to be addressing. If you assign an oral book report, who is supposed to listen? Just you, the teacher? If you are the only one grading a speech and the only one whose attention matters, you are wasting the time of the other twenty-nine students in the classroom. Please don't assign a speech that has no value to the listeners and requires no evaluation from them. (See Chapter 15 for more about student evaluation.) At a minimum, students should understand that they must design the speech for their peers, not just for you.

Beyond that, the list of questions about the audience for a class presentation will differ only slightly from those in Figure 3.1. In a classroom, the questions may seem easy to answer. For example, to answer the first four questions in Figure 3.1, we know that the audience members are all thirteen years old with a seventh-grade education and are evenly split between males and females. But those answers, while simple, have important implications. What is appropriate content for thirteen-year-olds in a school? Some parts of some topics may not be suitable for that age group. The sex education instruction in a class in fifth grade, for instance, is not the same as in a health class in eleventh grade, and it may be important to discuss with students the need to be appropriate for the age level.

The remaining questions in Figure 3.1 are also vital for effective communication. What does the audience already know about the topic? If the class has spent six weeks studying biomes, I can make some assumptions about background knowledge as I prepare a presentation of my desert diorama. I won't need to define what a biome is, nor will I need to explain many of the terms I use (e.g., *ecosystem*). Students should also ask themselves what the class wants from the speech. Do they need general information or specific information about a small part of the topic? Should they be motivated to act? If so, the speech must be persuasive, not just informational. Do they want to know how the topic will affect their lives? Then the relevant impact will be more important than the random facts that fill many student speeches. Finally, it's important for students to think carefully about the interests of students in the audience. These interests probably include Facebook, cell phones, iPods, friends, text messages, shopping, and sports practices, to name a few. They all have potential for linking the content of the speech to the interests of the audience. If students want to connect with an audience (and they *do* want to connect with the audience), they must search for ways to relate the topic to the interests of the audience so they can earn and hold their attention. Student speakers can't make those references unless they take time to learn about the audience.

HOW AUDIENCE ANALYSIS AFFECTS CLASS PRESENTATIONS

Imagine the following situation: In Classroom A an eighth-grade civics teacher tells students they will have to research a landmark Supreme Court case and give a speech about the case *in class*. He tells the students the speeches have to be five minutes long but doesn't give much more guidance than that. Can you predict what will happen? The students will dutifully look up information, copy it, give a speech full of words they don't understand, and look at their notes and occasionally at the teacher during the speech. Their classmates will be bored to tears.

In Classroom B, an eighth-grade civics teacher tells students they will have to research a landmark Supreme Court case and give a speech about the case *to the class*. Further, the teacher helps the students analyze the audience. She explains that the listeners are thirteen years old with no law school experience, so language has to be seriously modified between the research stage and the speaking stage. She explains that the audience is unfamiliar with history, so context events must be explained. The teacher reminds students that, because the class has been studying the court system for four weeks, they can assume that their classmates already know many things about the topic. It will not be necessary to explain how a case gets to the Supreme Court, for example. The teacher suggests that the audience only has a slight interest in the case students are going to present. They will only start to care if they know how the case affects their lives.

For instance, in a case about illegal search and seizure, the teacher suggests posing a question about whether it should be legal to take a student's cell phone and look at the text messages. The teacher builds into the rubric a category for "audience" and explains to the students that they will be scored on how well they gear the speech toward the audience. The speeches in Classroom B will be significantly more successful than the speeches in Classroom A.

You can easily see what made the speeches in Classroom B more successful. The teacher was explicit about how to analyze the audience. She helped students think of the key characteristics of the audience, gave specific advice to assist the students in making adjustments, and provided an example to demonstrate how to fit a speech to the class. You need to go through a similar process every time you give an assignment that requires oral communication.

The process of audience analysis gets quicker after the initial introduction of the concept. For example, the next time Teacher B prepares students for a speech assignment, she may only briefly remind them how to analyze their audience: "Tomorrow we will have our discussion on the novel. Remember during the discussion that the audience is the class, not me. Think of all we discussed before the Supreme Court speeches. Think of the qualities of your audience and gear your discussion comments toward the audience."

To help students become more adept at analyzing audiences, I recommend that at some point during the school year you change the audience for students' public speaking. You might have class buddies from another grade listen. Perhaps you invite parents to attend a poetry café or to judge the science fair presentations. In every instance, remind students that analyzing the audience is a skill they will need for their entire lives.

DISCUSSION IDEAS

1. Ask students to compare and contrast how they speak to their peers and to their parents. Ask questions like these: *What changes as the audience shifts? Do you speak differently to Dad than you do to Mom? How and why?* You might share some examples from your own life, such as how and why teachers speak differently in the teacher's lounge than they do in the classroom.

2. Create several hypothetical audiences. Tell students they will be speaking to a school assembly, a women's book club, a classroom from a different grade level, or whatever else you may come up with. Ask them to consider what adjustments they would make in a speech directed to a whole-school assembly as opposed to one prepared for a class of students the same age. Ask, for example, *How should a speech to the book club differ from a speech to the entire class?*

3. With students, look at real-life situations, such as the following candidate debate in front of a national television audience:

   MODERATOR: The national debt is now at X trillion dollars. What will you do about this problem?

   CANDIDATE A: As a percent of GDP, the debt is at its highest ratio since 1945. The ratio has doubled in the last two years alone. Annual deficits have ballooned from 200 billion to 1.6 trillion since 1992. Raising marginal tax rates and decreasing the rate of growth of entitlements is our only option.

   CANDIDATE B: Well, as I look at this great country, I see the blue Pacific Ocean to the west and the bustling cities on the Atlantic Ocean to the east. In between is the greatest country on the face of the earth. We have a great history. We have great people. No problem is too big for us. We can solve the deficit problem.

   Pose these questions: *What does Candidate A believe about the audience?* (The electorate is, by and large, logical and interested in facts and details.) *What does Candidate B believe about the audience?* (The electorate is emotional and prefers generalities to specifics.) *Which one is correct about this audience? Would your opinion change if the debate was in front of the American Economics Association?*

As you can see, real-life examples can bring up engaging discussions as students attempt to delineate audience and its implications.

[Activities 1, 2, 8, 10, and 16 from Chapter 16 can be used with this section.]

CHAPTER 4:

Content: Making the Message Valuable

There are six basic questions that will guide students in their search for appropriate content:

1. What is the purpose of the speech?
2. What content is required?
3. What is the engaging content?
4. What content should be clarified for my specific audience?
5. What connectors should be included to hook the audience members?
6. What content should be excluded?

Let's take a look at what we need to teach so that students can use these questions to build a successful speech.

THE PURPOSE

Now that I understand the audience, what do I say to them? Begin by thinking about the purpose of the speech. In school settings, almost all speeches assigned are informational speeches. The students are supposed to teach us about the contents of a book (book report), explain the features of a biome (presenting the biome diorama to us), share the essential developments in the Iraq War (current events newscast), and so on.

As teachers, we are often reluctant to allow anything in our classes that does not impart information. This is unfortunate. Students may grow from thinking differently, and a speech with a divergent purpose could fuel that growth. Assigning a speech with the purpose to entertain expands students' minds, allows a range of students to shine, and improves the classroom atmosphere. All of those objectives are important. Whatever the purpose for the speech you assign, be sure you share the goal with students. Don't assume they will intuitively understand.

THE REQUIRED CONTENT

For the most part, teachers specify the content of the speech. We tell students that, at a minimum, the book report must include the genre of the book, the main characters, the plot, and so on. The speech about a Supreme Court case must include the date of the case, the decision, why the case was important, and a quotation from the majority opinion. Notice the use of the phrase "at a minimum." We need to make clear that content guidelines are just that, guidelines. Although the speech *must* include those things, including *only* those things will not be sufficient. All speeches must also include interesting content and attention-holding elements.

When I was in the classroom, students would sometimes give what I referred to as the "checklist speech." They dutifully told me the name and date of a Supreme Court case, for example, and read a quote from the majority opinion. They checked off all the minimum requirements. Such speeches were completely forgettable, and listeners had a hard time paying attention. To avoid these situations, we must discuss ways to make content engaging.

CHOOSING ENGAGING CONTENT

It all starts with this truth: if you want the audience to be interested in what you are saying, *you* need to be interested in what you are saying. It is amazing how many students miss this point. No student will succeed unless *he or she* cares about the content. I have had students complain that the topic was assigned to them and that they weren't interested in it. I never accepted that excuse. There are fascinating details to share about the Supreme Court, the desert biome, *Tom Sawyer*, current events, or any other assigned topic. It is the speaker's job to find the engaging and intriguing information. Not all information is equal. Some facts will resonate and some will be forgotten. Have students consider questions like these: *What content is essential for the audience? What content would be meaningful for this audience?* For the most part, the speaker has the same background as audience members when we are in the school setting. We can ask students, *If you were listening to this speech, would you be interested and engaged?* This is a point that has to be made before the speech is built.

CLARIFIERS

Remind students that the reason we initially gather information about the audience is to make it possible to tailor the content of the speech specifically to that group. In some cases, we need to clarify content. Maybe we need to define some words that this group would not be familiar with. Maybe we need to explain the context of some events. A speech that mentions Vietnam War protests has little value for students who are unfamiliar with the Vietnam War and the feelings it generated among Americans. Remind students to ask themselves, *What do I need to explain to ensure that the listeners understand the meaning?*

CONNECTORS

Speeches are most effective if the listeners believe the speech was designed specifically for them. Think of the example from Chapter 3 about the Supreme Court speech on search and seizure. Students are familiar with cell phones. To connect the case to their experience, the teacher suggested using a cell phone analogy. She wanted the speaker to make a reference to something in the audience's culture. Another way to connect is to use an anecdote about a person the audience can relate to or a person they know. Speakers should use their knowledge of the audience to find the connectors that will bridge the gap between their topics and the lives of the listeners.

WHAT TO EXCLUDE

The content of a speech should be guided not only by what needs to be *included* but also by what needs to be *excluded*. Students often struggle to sort essential information from nonessential information. In the sample Supreme Court speech assignment, is it important that the case was decided on February 12, 1964? Would we be satisfied knowing only that it was decided in 1964? Do we need to know the names of all the justices who voted for the decision? You might say, "Obviously not," but this detail may not be obvious to your students. "The Court granted *certiorari* on April 11." "Certiorari"? Who knows what that means? And if you do know, do you care what date it was? Yes, the information was on the Web site you looked at, but that doesn't mean it has value in your speech.

There is another kind of nonessential content, something I call a "verbal virus." Unfortunately, verbal viruses seem to spread. Phrases such as "you know," "okay?," "know what I'm sayin'?," "all," and the ubiquitous "like" infect speaking. How many times have you heard these empty phrases?

> He was, like, all upset that they didn't like read him his rights, you know, so he like goes to court and they're all, yes, you gotta let him know.

> I want to tell you about the deficit, okay? We owe, like, trillions of dollars, okay? We need to do something, okay?

You've heard such blather too many times, right? Yet teachers almost never specifically explain the importance of eliminating these viruses from the content of a speech. Although it is true that these words will probably not be written in the text of a speech, we still must caution students about adding them to an oral presentation. These viruses are in a different category than the nervous tics such as "um" and "uh," which I will discuss later. The verbal viruses aren't the result of nerves but rather of fashion: it is just the cool way to speak at the moment. You would certainly correct students who included "ain't" in their speeches, and you must also correct students who improperly use "like." It is not sufficient to note a comment on the score sheet *after* the speech. The teaching is needed *before* the speech.

ORGANIZING THE ESSENTIALS

Now that we've examined the importance of teaching students to answer the six questions about content, let's look at how a student might answer those questions for a particular speech. In this example, a student has outlined content for a speech on a Supreme Court case about educating illegal immigrants.

1. What is the purpose of the speech?
   To inform classmates about a major Supreme Court decision and explain how it affects their lives today.
2. What content is required?
   a. *Name of case:* Plyler v. Doe
   b. *Date of case: 1982*
   c. *Decision of case: States must give free public education to illegal immigrant children because the Fourteenth Amendment says "all persons" must receive "equal protection under the law." The amendment does not say "all citizens," and illegal immigrants are persons.*
   d. *Why the decision was important: There are twelve million illegal immigrants in America, and lots of money is spent on them.*
   e. *Quote from the decision: "Education has a fundamental role in maintaining the fabric of our society. We cannot ignore the significant social costs borne by our Nation when select groups are denied the means to absorb the values and skills upon which our social order rests."*
3. What is the engaging content?
   With the money Texas could save if they didn't have to educate illegal aliens, they could buy every legal student a new MacBook each year. They could buy 30 million Flip video cameras, one for every resident of Texas. They could build 120 new high schools a year. They could hire 130,000 new teachers.
4. What content should be clarified?
   The Fourteenth Amendment needs to be explained. Its original purpose and the time frame in which it was adopted are important.
5. What connectors should be included?
   Our state has a lot of illegal immigrants.
   Our parents pay taxes to the school district, and their money goes

to educate illegal immigrants.

     Our class sizes are bigger because of money spent on illegal immigrants instead of more teachers, and by spending money on illegal immigrants, we have less money for new computers and textbooks.

     When you get a job, you will pay taxes that go to educate illegal immigrants.

6. What content should be excluded?

   Specific names: the names of all the justices, attorneys
   Specific dates: months and days
   Lower court decisions
   Legal terms, unless they are important and explained
   Verbal virus "like," which I say a lot

We always ask students to prewrite before they begin a writing assignment, so it should not be thought of as unusual to require some preparatory steps before they deliver a speech. This is a way to use speaking assignments to reinforce writing instruction. Ask students to write out the answers to the six questions about content and submit them to you for approval. With these answers in hand, each student can begin to build something more than the "checklist" speech.

DISCUSSION IDEAS

1. Discuss with students a hypothetical speech about the school lunchroom. First, have students imagine that the purpose is to inform the audience about nutrition in the cafeteria foods. Ask, *How does that control content?* Next, have the students imagine that the purpose is to entertain. Ask, *How does that change the content? What will be in the first speech? What will be in the second speech?*

2. Ask several students to give a short, impromptu speech about a simple topic, such as a favorite activity or favorite movie. (Be sure to create an atmosphere that demands tolerance, encourages bravery, and fosters the ability to laugh at oneself. Impromptu speeches are difficult, and students will make mistakes. I discuss more about class atmosphere in Chapter 8.) After the speech, ask the class to discuss the verbal viruses: *How many times did you hear "like," "you know," or "okay"?*

3. Have students imagine a hypothetical topic, such as "Caring for Dogs," and have them assume the audience is a group of first graders. Ask, *What should be included in the speech to connect to that audience?* Then have students assume the audience is a group of veterinarians. Ask, *What would that speech include? What would be included in the first-grader speech that would be left out of the veterinarians' speech? What would you include for the doctors that you would not include for six-year-olds?*

4. Discuss adding content to make a speech interesting. Use questions like these: *What could be added to a speech about the International Space Station to make it interesting to our class? What would you have to include in a speech about national health care to hold the attention of the class?*

[Activities 1, 2, 3, 7, 8, 10, 13, and 16 from Chapter 16 can be used with this section.]

CHAPTER 5:

Organization: Making the Speech Easy to Follow

An old cliché found in nearly every book about public speaking gives this advice to speakers: Tell your audience what you're going to tell them; tell them; then tell them what you told them. That is the most common organizational form. For example:

Today I will tell you the three reasons why I love cats, I will tell you how to care for a cat, and I will show you pictures of my cat doing funny things.

The first reason why I love cats is . . . The second reason I love cats is . . . The third reason I love cats is . . .

To care for cats, remember that cats need fresh water every day. Also, . . .

And, finally, here is a picture of my cat stuck in the handle of the grocery bag . . .

So now you know why I love cats, how to care for cats, and the funny things they do.

The formula is based on a simple truth: people do not listen well. To aid listeners, speakers have to make very clear what the audience will need to listen for during the speech, and speakers need to remind the audience immediately about what they have just heard in order to reinforce the message. That formula is a very good starting place for your class instruction about organizing a speech. The formula also makes clear that a speech needs an introduction, body, and conclusion. But building a truly powerful speech takes more.

GRABBER OPENINGS

Often, students start a speech with, "Hi, my name is Skippy, and I am going to tell you about my book, *The Gospel According to Larry.*"

"Hi, my name is . . ." is a terrible way to start a speech. It is unacceptable, even if a speech is designed to introduce the speaker. For example, I watched elementary students give brown bag speeches at the beginning of the school year as a way of introducing themselves to their classmates. The speeches involved paper lunch bags with items inside that represented important things in each student's life: a picture of the family dog, a mini soccer ball to represent a favorite sport, a controller for a favorite gaming system, and so on. It may seem acceptable to have students introduce themselves at the beginning of the brown bag speech and similar speeches, but even then, more is required.

A speech should start with an opening that grabs the audience's attention and makes the listeners want to hear more. The opening should be smooth, short, and dynamic. All audiences will give the speaker a moment of attention out of curiosity. Speakers have to take that initial curiosity and convert it to longer-term interest. They must wake up the audience. Engage them. Do something to ensure that the audience will stay with them for more than the opening minute.

There are several ways speakers can grab the attention of the audience:

The challenge. For example:
Today I am going to ask you to do something very difficult, but something that will change the world.

The provocative question. For example:
What would you do if you had no money and your family was starving? Would robbery be justified?

The powerful quote. A relevant quotation from a renowned person can be effective. The quote loses impact, however, if the audience does not know the author of the quote and does not recognize the author as an authority in the area.

The surprising statistic. For example:
The average Internet user spends fewer than ten seconds on a Web page before moving on.

The unusual fact. For example:
There is a garbage patch the size of Texas floating in the middle of the Pacific Ocean. It is made up of plastic and debris that has been caught in currents in the ocean.

The poignant story. Sometimes a powerful and touching personal story can be used to tug at the heartstrings of the audience. This makes the subsequent factual presentation more engaging.

The unexpected. For example:
I have been multitasking for my entire life. I am always doing several things at once: texting, listening to music, surfing the Web, homework. I believe multitasking has ruined my brain.

The teaser. For example:
Three minutes from now, I will tell you something that you will never forget as long as you live.
(Of course, the speaker will have to deliver as promised.)

Why not brainstorm ideas with your students and model grabber openings?
For the brown bag speech:

(Pulling out a mini soccer ball.) I live for this! I am a soccer maniac. Forget school. Let's play soccer! My name is Ronaldo, and I want to tell you about myself.

Do you know what is in this bag? Me! I am in there. I am Kristen, and this is my life.

For the *Larry* oral book report:

How many of you use some social media site? Facebook? MySpace? Have you ever lied on a post you made for the site? You don't have to answer that, but Josh, the main character in my book, lied. A lot."

They own you. You wear what they want you to wear, you eat what they tell you to eat, and you watch what they want you to watch. Corporations like Nike, McDonald's, and Apple control you. Larry knows that.

What would you change about yourself if you could? Want to be taller? Thinner? Richer? Better at math? Better at some sport? Want to start your life over and rebuild yourself? Well, that is exactly what Josh did. He is the main character of The Gospel According to Larry.

It is always useful to ask the speechwriter to trade places, mentally, with the listener. Ask students to consider this question: *If you heard that opening, would you be interested?*

ORGANIZATIONAL STRATEGIES

Certainly, the outline of a speech has to include the key information, the required elements (as we discussed in Chapter 4). As we build a speech, we also need to ask what the basic method of organizing that information will be. There are a few basic structures:

- chronological/sequential
- problem and solution
- compare and contrast
- topical
- geographical

- order of importance

Chronological/Sequential Organization

For an oral book report, the speech most likely will flow chronologically. The beginning of the speech will include what happened first in the book, and the end will discuss what happened at the end. A speech about the Civil War also most likely will be in chronological order, moving from events that occurred in 1861 to events that occurred in 1862, and so on. Filling in the outline is easy for this sort of speech:

I. 1861, causes of the war
  a. states' rights
  b. expansion of slavery
II. Early battles
III. Gettysburg and other major battles

Problem and Solution Organization

Some speeches don't follow a time line. Often, teachers assign a problem and solution speech. In these assignments, students are supposed to research an issue affecting us and propose solutions. Generally, they should organize the speech by explaining the problem and then introducing the solutions. A student discussing acid rain, for example, would define acid rain, explain its causes, discuss its impact, and then offer ideas for stopping the causes and/or alleviating the damages of acid rain.

Compare and Contrast Organization

A compare and contrast speech forces a different organizational structure. Usually, a list of similarities is followed by a list of differences. In a language arts class, a student might be asked to compare two characters in a story. In a civics class, a student might be asked to do a presentation about two different bills proposed in Congress for solving the illegal immigration problem. Instead of describing all the details of one and then describing all the details of the other, it would be easier to group the similarities and differences. For the civics assignment, the speech might look like this:

The House bill is in some ways like the Senate bill. Both bills have the goal of stopping the flow of illegal immigrants. The bill in the House says . . . and the Senate bill says . . . Second, both bills want to put penalties on employers who hire illegal immigrants. The House bill says employers would be . . . and the Senate bill has almost the exact same language. Finally, both bills want to offer illegal immigrants already here a way to become citizens. The House version says illegals could become citizens by . . .

There are some big differences, though. The bill in the House of Representatives proposes spending fourteen billion dollars to build a 750-mile-long fence at the border. The Senate bill does not include money for a fence . . .

Topical Organization

Topical speeches ask the speaker to focus on ideas that are somehow related. For example, a speaker might describe twenty-first century skills for students. He or she could begin with a discussion of collaboration skills, move to a discussion of Internet literacy skills, then continue with a discussion of Web publishing skills, and so on. No particular order works best.

Geographical Organization

Speeches can be organized geographically if the topic lends itself to this. A student might first speak about the northeast part of the country, then the east, and then the southeast; or speak about the animals of the desert, then move to the plains; or speak about the committee rooms and what happens there and then talk about the floor of the entire legislative chamber. With geographically organized speeches, the listener visualizes the locations and mentally organizes the information.

Order of Importance Organization

Persuasive speeches have the goal of moving the audience to some conclusion. The speaker presents a series of ideas that compels listeners to agree with him. For example, if a student wants to persuade the class to sign a petition to change the menu choices in the school cafeteria, he might first list all the reasons he could think of that would persuade students to sign the petition. Once he had the list, he would whittle it down to the three best reasons and decide which of the three is the most persuasive and which is the least persuasive.

Three is the magic number in persuasive speeches. Listeners cannot hold many ideas in their heads at one time, and including more than three reasons will increase forgetfulness and decrease effectiveness. The standard way of organizing persuasive speeches is to open with what you believe is your second best idea, continue with your third best idea, and save the best argument for last. Why? The last words you say are freshest in the minds of the listeners and easiest to recall. Because of initial curiosity (and a grabber opening), the first words you say will be more memorable too. This is another time students can make good use of the audience analysis: What would this group think is the best argument, the most persuasive? That will be the last point made.

Oddly, a humorous speech is similar in structure to a persuasive speech. To move the audience to laughter, speakers should open with their second funniest line or story. Save the best for last.

SIGNPOSTS

All speeches, no matter the type, require skillful transitions between ideas. I have had success using the term *signposts* in discussing transitions with students. Here is the analogy: Take a drive down any interstate highway. You are continually met by large, green signs: "Kalamazoo 47 miles," "Kalamazoo 32 miles," "Kalamazoo 16 miles," "Kalamazoo 2 miles," "Kalamazoo next 4 exits." At no time are you unaware of your location or goal. That's what signposts do: they tell you where you are and where you are going. Signposts in a speech should do the same thing. Recall the basic formula for organizing a speech (tell the audience what you're going to tell them; tell them; then tell them what you told them). This is really a way of using signposts to let your audience know where you are going, where you are, and where you have been.

Often, students resist the idea of including such obvious markers. They think it is awkward to insert signposts. The truth is, though, that most people listen less well than they read, and a speaker must be overly clear in order to be followed well. Listeners get more out of a speech if they have specific signposts along the way.

At the basic level, signposts are numeric:

You have just been diagnosed with a serious disease. Because your father lost his job, your family has no health insurance. What happens? If you live in America, you die. If you live in the Netherlands, you live. Today I want to give you three reasons why we need national health care. First, there are . . . Second, too many . . .

Although the preceding speech is not sophisticated, it includes well-marked reasons that are easy to recall at the end of the speech. The listener knows from the outset to be looking for three reasons and does not need to wonder if what he or she just heard was one of the reasons.

At a more advanced level, signposts, like transitions in writing, become more fluid:

You have just been diagnosed with a serious disease. Because your father lost his job, your family has no health insurance. What happens? If you live in America, you die. If you live in the Netherlands, you live. Today, I want to give you three reasons why we need national health care. Let's begin by looking at the number of . . . I want to move on to another important argument . . . I believe my final point will persuade those of you who remain unsure . . .

POWERFUL CLOSING

Once students finish the body of the speech, they have to build a conclusion. I have heard far too many student speeches end with, "And that's my speech." Ugh. That's why we need to help students figure out how to end a speech. Recall the basic format for any speech. One option for a conclusion is to "tell them what you told them." The speaker simply reiterates or highlights the main points. This option should be familiar from writing lessons. Like the concluding sentence of a paragraph or the concluding paragraph of an essay, this kind of speech ending is summative:

> *To conclude, I want to review my three reasons for national health care: to eliminate waste and save money, to help the poor, and to save lives. Now you understand.*

At a more advanced level, the speaker may want to leave listeners with one memorable thought—one key unforgettable concept:

> *Though I have presented four reasons for national health care, I want you to focus on this one idea: A child somewhere in America will die today due to a lack of health care. A child will die. Can you live with that?*

In some instances, a call to action is required:

> *We cannot sit back and let innocent people die. You must tell your parents to call their congressional representatives. You must join organizations that support health care reform. You must do what you can to end the deaths.*

In addition, think back to the previous suggestions for grabber openings. Those techniques can be used to craft powerful closings as well. A challenge, a quotation, or a poignant story can effectively wrap up a speech, engaging listeners until the very end. Under no circumstances should a speech just stop—but students won't know that unless we specifically instruct them.

BRINGING TOGETHER THE CONTENT AND ORGANIZATION

Reflecting on all the parts of the speech, we can now go back and expand the list of questions we asked students to think about in Chapter 4. Indeed, you may want to require a writing assignment, such as an outline or brief answers to questions, at this point in the process. The completed assignment for our sample speech might look like this:

1. What opening will you use?

   There are twelve million illegal immigrants in our country. That's three times as many people as the entire population of Colorado. Twelve million criminals. They all get free health care and schooling because of the Supreme Court case I will present today.

2. What kind of organization will you use?

   Chronological: the situation that led to the case; the decision of the case; how the decision affected Texas afterward; what the decision means today

3. What is the purpose of the speech?

   To inform classmates about a major Supreme Court decision and explain how it affects their lives today.

4. What content is required?

   a. *Name of case:* Plyler v. Doe

   b. *Date of case: 1982*

   c. *Decision of case: States must give free public education to illegal immigrant children because the Fourteenth Amendment says "all persons" must receive "equal protection under the law." The amendment does not say "all citizens," and illegal immigrants are persons.*

   d. *Why the decision was important: There are twelve million illegal immigrants in America, and lots of money is spent on them.*

   e. *Quote from the decision: "Education has a fundamental role in maintaining the fabric of our society. We cannot ignore the significant social costs borne by our Nation when select groups are denied the means to absorb the values and skills upon which our social order rests."*

5. What is the engaging content?

   With the money Texas could save if they didn't have to educate illegal aliens, they could buy every legal student a new MacBook each year. They could buy 30 million Flip video cameras, one for every resident of Texas. They could build 120 new high schools a year. They could hire 130,000 new teachers.

6. What signposts will you use?

   a. *To begin, let me explain what was happening in Texas that led to the lawsuit...*

   b. *Now that you know the situation, here is what happened in the Court...*

   c. *That's what the Court said. What did it mean to Texas?...*

   d. *So that is what it meant and how it affected Texas. But it also affects us...*

7. What content should be clarified?

   The Fourteenth Amendment needs to be explained. Its original purpose and the time frame in which it was adopted are important.

8. What connectors should be included?

   a. *Our state has a lot of illegal immigrants.*

   b. *Our parents pay taxes to the school district, and their money goes to educate illegal immigrants.*

   c. *Our class sizes are bigger because of money spent on illegal immigrants instead of more teachers, and by spending money on illegal immigrants, we have less money for new computers and textbooks.*

   d. *When you get a job, you will pay taxes that go to educate illegal immigrants.*

9. What content should be excluded?

   a. *Specific names: the names of all the justices, attorneys*

   b. *Specific dates: months and days*

   c. *Lower court decisions*

   d. *Legal terms, unless they are important and explained*

   e. *Verbal virus "like," which I say a lot*

10. How will you end the speech?

    Twelve million. Remember? Twelve million criminals. They aren't in jail, they are in our schools. They aren't being deported, they are in our hospitals. All because of the decision in Plyler v. Doe.

DISCUSSION IDEAS

1. Pose several topic ideas for class discussion. Have students share ideas for openings by asking questions like these: *How can you introduce your classmate beyond saying, "Hi, this is Jamal"? How would you open a speech about the book* Elijah of Buxton*? How would you start a book report on the book* Numbers*? How could you grab the audience's attention when you present your desert biome diorama? If you want to persuade us that multitasking is bad for students, what would be an effective opening for that talk?*

2. Teach a lesson about transitional phrases. Make a list of options students can choose from:

   For a chronological/sequential speech:
   > *afterward, before, then, once, next, last, at last, at length, first, second, (and so on), at first, formerly, rarely, usually, another, finally, soon, meanwhile, afterward, generally, in order to, subsequently, previously, in the meantime, immediately, eventually, concurrently, simultaneously*

   For a compare and contrast speech:
   > *on the contrary, contrarily, notwithstanding, but, however, nevertheless, in spite of, in contrast, yet, on one hand, on the other hand, rather, or, nor, conversely, at the same time, while this may be true*

   For a topical speech:
   > *and; in addition to; furthermore; moreover; besides; too; also; both; another; equally important; first, second, (and so on); again; further; last; finally; not only; but also; as well as; in the second place; next; likewise; similarly; in fact; as a result; consequently; in the same way; for example; for instance; however; thus; therefore; otherwise*

3. Brainstorm endings as a class. Use actual topics from the class. Use questions like these: *How could Kevin finish this speech? What should Maria do to make her ending powerful?*

[Activities 1, 2, 7, and 16 from Chapter 16 can be used with this section.]

CHAPTER 6:

Visual Aids: Enhancing the Words

M any speakers like using visual aids. For the beginning speaker, I recommend *not* using visual aids. Often the visual aid is merely something to hide behind. I think students benefit more by being front and center.

In addition, visual aids can become a distraction in two significant ways. First, preparing a visual aid takes focus away from preparing the speech. Students typically spend a significant amount of time preparing a PowerPoint presentation or poster and not enough time building a meaningful speech. If I have allotted a week of preparation before a speech, I don't want students spending six days tinkering with the font style. Second, visual aids can distract the listener. Rather than focus on the speaker, the audience focuses on the visual aid, and the speaker becomes subordinate to the picture. Why would I want to build an attention-diverter into my speech?

Having said that, I know teachers love to assign visual aids, so I may not win the argument. Indeed, it would not be possible to give some speeches without visual aids. Recall the brown bag speeches mentioned on pages 37–38. The visual aids were necessary (and adorable). Yet, as with every other aspect of speaking, students need meaningful and specific instruction about using visual aids. Don't assume students know how to develop them. Too often students copy a diagram or picture straight from the one book they used. (Did I say book? That's being overly optimistic! I meant straight from whatever Web site they clicked on.) They often fail to analyze the appropriateness of the image.

FOUR CRITERIA FOR VISUAL AIDS

Visual aids need to meet four criteria. They must be relevant, important, accessible, and simple. Have you ever seen a speech where the student brings in his *Star Wars* light saber and waves it around, saying, "The Second Amendment gives us the right to bear arms, and that is what I am going to talk about today"? Unfortunately, I have. No discussion of the Second Amendment has ever centered on light sabers. The toy is totally irrelevant. As a grabber, it probably does get our attention, but it makes us think of Jabba the Hutt and R2-D2 instead of the crucial constitutional issues.

In every speech, the visual aid should be based on the purpose of the talk. If the speaker wants to argue against a broad interpretation of the Second Amendment, a graph showing gun deaths in the United States compared to gun deaths in other countries would be relevant. If the speaker wants to inform us about the origins of the Second Amendment, pictures of the Redcoats and Colonists with muskets might be useful.

In addition to being relevant, visual aids should be important; they are redundant if they merely repeat what the speaker says. A poster that has bullet points of the four ways water gets polluted is only marginally useful in a speech where the speaker has just told us four ways water gets polluted. No visual aid should be presented unless it illustrates something crucial that we would not otherwise clearly understand.

Imagine a student giving a speech about water pollution. She brings in a picture of a river. Yes, the image may be relevant to the topic, but is it important? Does it add significant information? A picture of a river that shows various pollutants flowing into it from acid rain, fertilizer runoff, and industrial waste would be vital to our understanding of the topic. When the student says that fertilizer runoff from farms and golf courses gets into our rivers, the audience probably doesn't know exactly how that happens. She might say that fertilizer concentration builds up and harms fish, but the audience might not know *how* fertilizer can harm fish. What kind of visual aid would help the audience understand how fertilizer gets from a golf course into a river or how fertilizer kills fish? An effective visual aid would be one that takes complex issues such as these and makes them easy to understand.

Visual aids also need to be accessible in two senses, mentally and visually. Think back to the analysis of the audience. If, for a speech about water pollution, I bring in a complex flowchart showing the chemical compounds in our water and how they got there, it may be relevant and important, but it would not help fourth graders understand the problem. Something simpler would be far more accessible to them. The visual aid must be on the same level as the audience—it has to be *mentally* accessible. Being accessible also includes being big enough, clear enough, vivid enough, and neat enough to be seen by everyone in the audience. Are the words and images just right for the size of the room? Do the colors work? Certainly, color is important to the impact of the visual aid, but fluorescent hot pink may not be the best choice. Visual aids need to be *visually* accessible.

That brings me to the final point: visual aids must be simple. Have you been to a workshop where the speaker projects several slides from a PowerPoint presentation, each with densely packed type, multiple bullet points, and complex flowcharts with arrows everywhere? Not very effective, right? Years ago, I was introduced to the U.S. military's KISS principle, and I imagine you have heard of it also. One version, "Keep it simple, stupid," seems a bit harsh in the school setting, but another version, "Keep it simple, students," should be introduced in our classrooms. For starters, students must be cautioned to design, not decorate. A visual aid is not an art project but rather a tool to enhance the listener's understanding. A visual aid should contain minimal text. A graph should be easy to follow. The visual aid must make a strong positive contribution to the speech, not distract audience members as they try to decipher it.

FINAL THOUGHTS ON VISUAL AIDS

Everything I have described in Part II, "Building a Speech," refers to what is done before the speaker ever says a word. Let me offer one bit of advice that relates to performing a speech but that probably should be mentioned as you explain visual aids to students. The visual aid should not be unveiled until the precise moment that the speaker wants the audience to focus on it. If a student displays the image before she begins speaking, the audience members will be distracted, wondering when the explanation of the picture will be forthcoming. They will be guessing in their own minds about what the picture means or what the speaker plans to do with it. Similarly, as soon as the speaker finishes with the visual aid, she should remove it from sight. If not, students in the audience will continue focusing on the aid and not the speaker, and side conversations discussing the artistic merits of the aid will result.

DISCUSSION IDEAS

1. Discuss responses to these questions with students: *What kind of speech might require a visual aid? What would be the purpose of the visual aid?* (Answers might include: speeches explaining processes, demonstration speeches, or speeches describing something that the audience needs to see pictured in order to understand. All have the purpose of clarifying the content.)
2. If you are making an assignment that requires a visual aid, choose a sample topic and discuss with students the kinds of visual aids that might be effective. For example, if you have assigned a book share, use a book that students are familiar with, and brainstorm ideas of the sorts of visual aids that would enhance a presentation on that book. This will model the process for your students.

[Activities 5, 6, and 12 from Chapter 16 can be used with this section.]

CHAPTER 7:

Appearance: Dressing for the Occasion

I realize that appearance might at first seem to be an odd fit in a section about building a speech. Let me explain my thought process. As I mentioned, before a speaker ever utters a word, she has to create the words that will be heard. She also has to create the visuals that will be seen. One of those may be a visual aid to increase the impact of the presentation. Another visual is the speaker herself. *She* will be seen, and s*he* will be judged before she ever opens her mouth. The speaker is, in a sense, a visual aid, too.

In some cases, teachers require a certain appearance. They might ask students to dress as a character from a novel for a book report or dress as a particular person from history for a biography presentation. Obviously, in those situations, students will have to create a costume to complete the building-the-speech stage. But even when costumes are not required, students should consider their appearance before they get to the podium.

A speaker must "build" an image to match the speech. You have realized this from your personal experiences (which I encourage you to share with your students). When you went to your job interview, for example, you prepared by considering how to dress. You may have sought advice: "Should I wear this?" "Is this too formal?" You probably went through the same thoughts as you got ready for back-to-school night. Let students know that you plan your appearance when you plan your speeches. Ask them to think about how a candidate might choose an outfit for a campaign speech. For instance, what does a male candidate wear for a speech at the Iowa Farm Bureau? Can students visualize it? Sleeves rolled up, no tie, possibly a hat. What does the candidate wear for a nationally televised debate? Probably a white shirt, dark suit, and red tie perfectly knotted. No speaker ignores appearance.

There is no reason to prepare a great speech only to have it diminished by poor appearance. To begin with, suggest that students choose their outfits to avoid annoying habits. (I will talk more about this in Chapter 8, "Poise.") Hooded sweatshirts are quite popular, but they offer the potential for distraction. I have often seen students twirling the strings of their hoodies. I have also watched them moving their hands in their front pockets in ways that reminded me of a scene from the movie *Alien*. Do you know the one I mean? An alien has inhabited the body of one of the humans on the base, and after some wriggling the alien head bursts out of the human's stomach. Don't let your students wear hoodies. I have watched students play with the cuff of a long sleeve and retract the hands into the sleeve, only to make them reappear later. Don't let them wear overly long sleeves. Many female students have hairstyles in which half of their faces are covered by bangs. In addition to hiding their faces from the audience (a bad idea), the hair style leads to annoying head jerks as students try to get the hair off their faces and out of their eyes. Inevitably the hair slides back down, necessitating another head jerk . . . and another and another. Don't let students show up on performance day without a hair band or barrette. Similarly, students with untucked shirts are somehow compelled to tug continuously at the bottom of their shirts. Don't allow them to leave their shirts untucked. Bottom line: the popular style in school at the moment may not be workable on presentation day.

Beyond those specific changes to avoid annoying habits, I believe that if you have a major presentation required in class, you must require a major change in dress code. Students need to know that what is acceptable on a normal day in class is not acceptable on the day of a big presentation. I got very few complaints from students when I required formal dress on presentation day. I explained that by "formal," I meant "the outfit you currently own that you think makes you look the most professional." When my sons were in middle school, they did not own a suit or a sports coat. For them, "formal" was the best pair of khakis they owned and a neatly pressed oxford shirt, which was a far cry from the jeans and T-shirts worn on a typical day. When I required formal dress for speeches, if you went out into the hall between classes, you could see which students were presenting that day. It was no big deal; it was just a fact of life in Mr. Palmer's classroom.

Changing the dress code changes the attitude of the speaker, which in turn changes the audience's perception of the speaker. Students know that an outfit can affect the way you feel. They know that clothes can make you feel confident and impressive. And they know that how you dress affects people's opinion of you. We absolutely *do* judge a book by its cover. In the real world, you alter your appearance to match the occasion. Why not have your students start practicing that now?

FINAL COMMENTS ON BUILDING A SPEECH

It is rare to find an individual of *any* age who can speak brilliantly off the cuff. Impromptu speaking is extremely difficult. Extemporaneous speaking involves at least a bit of warning and gives the speaker time to jot down some notes, but it, too, is hard to master. In my experience, most students are not successful if they just try to wing it or rely on a brief outline. For these reasons, I recommend that you require a written script. While you may treat the script as a writing assignment and grade it as such, don't feel compelled to do so. I never had time to grade all the texts for all the speeches I assigned, nor did I feel it was necessary. Students should create written texts because they are crucial to delivering great speeches, and the focus should be on the oral presentation, not the written work. I did ask to *see* my students' scripts before their presentations, but I looked for the elements of building a speech, not mechanics, paragraphing, and so on.

Although it is highly unlikely that students will deliver their speeches exactly as written, they must nonetheless complete the writing. (In Chapter 11, I discuss using the text during the performance.) Christopher Witt, a speech consultant and author of *Real Leaders Don't Do PowerPoint* (2009) has estimated that a five-minute speech contains 750 words. That's not an unreasonable amount of writing for students. The text allows students to verify that they have all the elements they need, the text gives them confidence, and writing the text helps them remember the speech come performance time. Studying the text visually improves performing it orally.

You may think that most of what I have written in this section applies only to a major presentation. Many teachers limit these to one a year: the seven-minute speech about the research paper; the four-minute opening statement for the formal debate; the culmination of the storytelling unit; the explanation of the science project. Although every speech may not require all of the writing that is needed to pull off a major presentation, each speech does require thinking about *all* of the elements of building a speech. Even a two-minute show-and-tell speech should be built with the audience in mind, with appropriate content that is well organized, with quality visual aids, and with consideration of how to dress for the performance. Students need to get in the habit of thinking about all of these elements every time they plan to speak. I was amazed at the way even routine class discussions improved by the end of the year in my classes when I reinforced this kind of thinking about public speaking. I knew that at the back of the students' minds, they were considering audience, content, organization, and building a quality response to the discussion question. And I knew they were also thinking about the other main part of public speaking: performing a speech.

PART III
PERFORMING A SPEECH

How a speech is performed may be more important than how it is built. If the speaker cannot deliver the speech well, no one will ever notice how well it was written. As Chris Witt points out, "Knowledge isn't power; communicating knowledge is" (2009, 5). The most brilliant ideas are worthless if the speaker can't deliver them. Let me give you two examples.

My children all graduated from the same high school. I heard the principal speak more times than I can recall at back-to-school nights, award ceremonies, PTO meetings, and other events. I almost never paid attention to what he said in those speeches because I was focused on his annoying habit of fidgeting with the height adjustment ring on the microphone stand. He simply could not leave that ring alone. The entire time he spoke, he would wiggle the ring back and forth with one hand while holding the mike with the other hand so it wouldn't slide down during the loosening part of his fidgeting. He probably had important information to impart about the workings of the school, or perhaps inspirational words for the honorees, but all I noticed was the microphone stand.

On the other hand, my own experience in high school proved to me that if a speech is delivered well, it is possible no one will notice how poor the content is. I am not advocating that students do what I did many years ago, but I did learn the importance of performance. We were supposed to have read a few chapters of *A Tale of Two Cities* for English. I hadn't done the assignment. (I assure you this was a rare occurrence. I was a model student generally. Really, I was.) I knew the odds were with me. How many students would get called on in one class? Six or seven out of thirty maybe, so I had only a one-in-five chance of being called upon. But I lost.

> TEACHER: Erik, what do you think?
>
> ERIK: (*Poised, confident, making eye contact, with feeling.*) I immediately sensed why the book is a tale of two cities. The word "tale" is so much more encompassing, more complex than the word "story," for example, and the early chapters have a richness that suggests the depths of the tale. But I was most intrigued by the juxtaposition of the two cities, the interplay of the events, and the characters in the two very different locales. I agree with Debbie that the personalities of the protagonists seem to adjust as the environment shifts. (*Debbie, who had spoken earlier, had read the book.*)

The teacher seemed satisfied with my response/bluff and went on to the next student. I apologize for seeming to glorify a situation in which I pulled the wool over a teacher's eyes. But I believe that students who speak better *do* get viewed differently. There were many times in my teaching career when I had to struggle to adjust my perception of a student—the *oral* student was so good that I had a hard time realizing that the *whole* student was needier than I initially thought.

It should be no surprise that actors often succeed in politics. They are performers, and, in an era of sound bites and video clips, performance is crucial. Voters tend to vote for the performance rather than the content. Is the candidate believable? Charismatic? Charming? How often does a performance error affect an election? In contrast, how often does a great performance sway voters? In a world of video conferences, Skype, and phones with video calling, performance becomes crucial to your students' futures as well. They will be judged on how well they deliver the sales pitch, the presentation to the board, the closing argument to the jury, the lesson to the class.

I realize that most people use the word *deliver* when discussing speeches, but I prefer the word *performance*. Delivery is just handing something over to someone. The FedEx guy delivers a package; the postal carrier delivers a letter; the speaker delivers a speech. No big deal, right? But delivering a speech *is* a big deal. It involves several skills that few people master in a lifetime. It is a performance art. The speaker is on stage and in the spotlight, if not literally, certainly figuratively. Even in small, informal speaking situations, the speaker is evaluated on performance elements. Sometimes the audience buys the performance and sometimes not. You've probably had an experience in which you thought, "He *said* he was going to do it, but I didn't believe him." Or perhaps the reverse occurred: "I can't believe she did that! She told me that we were in agreement, yet she went to her friend and said the exact opposite." You judged the performance. In the first case, something about the performance made you doubt the words. In the second case, the performance fooled you into believing a lie. Performance counts.

The performance aspect of speaking can be broken into six parts: poise, voice, life, eye contact, gestures, and speed. Many years ago, I made a poster for my class listing those elements (see figure on next page). The capital letters stood out, and PVLEGS became a simple mnemonic for remembering the parts of performance. That mnemonic has surprised me in its appeal. As I moved from the elementary school to the middle school, students still found PVLEGS useful. I assumed high school students would find it childish, but that didn't turn out to be true. I suppose that Roy G. Biv may seem like an odd name, but millions of students (and adults) remember the colors of the rainbow because of that name. Similarly, while PVLEGS may sound odd, it represents all the elements needed to become a master orator.

Poise
- Appear calm and confident
- Avoid distracting behaviors

Voice
- Speak every word clearly
- Use a volume level just right for the space

Life
- Express passion and emotions with your voice

Eye Contact
- Connect visually with the audience
- Look at each audience member

Gestures
- Use hand motions
- Move your body
- Have an expressive face

Speed
- Talk with appropriate speed: not too fast, not too slow
- Use pauses for effect and emphasis

Six Trait Speaking™
pvlegs.com

© Erik Palmer

CHAPTER 8:

Poise: Appearing Calm and Confident

I f you check the library or search online, you will find many books and articles about overcoming the fear of public speaking. Almost all of the articles will include phrases similar to these:

Statistics show that public speaking is the number one fear of adults.

According to statistics, fear of speaking ranks higher in people's minds than the fear of death.

According to national surveys, fear of public speaking ranks among Americans' top fears, surpassing fear of heights, fear of flying, and fear of terrorism.

None of the articles or books actually cite the source of the "statistics." It seems highly unlikely that anyone would choose to die if asked whether they would prefer to give a speech or to be put to death. But the point is clear: many people fear giving a speech. The fear of public speaking is greatly overstated, though. In spite of the terror and dread that is supposedly out there, I have never had one student fail to give an assigned speech. Not one. Every student (and every adult) I have worked with has been successful at performing the speech when the time came. Not all were master orators, but all were able to overcome their fears.

GETTING BEYOND THE BUTTERFLIES

The truth is that *all* speakers have a degree of nervousness. Even a professional speaker with massive experience will have a heightened level of excitement before a presentation. It is also true that if that nervousness is obvious, listeners can be distracted and miss the point of the speech. This is why the first skill needed in performing a speech is poise. Webster defines poise as an "easy, self-possessed assurance of manner . . . pleasantly tranquil" (Merriam-Webster 1998, 899). The key to performing a speech is to *appear* calm and assured even when we may not feel precisely that way (or even remotely close to it).

All of us have normal reactions to stressful situations. First, acknowledge these reactions. Let students know that what they feel is normal and expected. Students can expect a dry mouth because saliva dries up. They can expect butterflies, a nervous, almost queasy feeling in the stomach. Shortness of breath is common, as is a rapid heart rate. Students may find they are sweating. Hands may tremble; knees may feel weak and wobbly; the voice may be unsteady and sound shaky. These symptoms may sound dreadful and dramatic, but assure students that they are typical reactions to being "on stage." Another normal response—perhaps less disturbing than these others—is the nervous smile. Students take the stage and begin with a grin on their faces; it doesn't matter what the topic is:

> Student: (*Smiling.*) Today, I want to tell you about the day my dog died . . .

These things happen. Tell students not to worry. Normalizing these symptoms of stress will take the charge out of them.

NOTICING OUR ANNOYING HABITS

Every speaker has some habit or distinguishing tick that is an outcome of nervousness. Yes, *every* speaker. Ask your students—they will tell you what *you* do. For the principal at my children's high school, it was fidgeting with the microphone. For beginning speakers, the list of annoying mannerisms can be quite long:

- A head flick to get the bangs out of the eyes
- Repeatedly saying "um," "and um," and "uh"
- Tugging at the hem of an untucked shirt
- Twirling hair next to the ear
- Jangling coins with a hand in the pocket
- Buckling one knee and then the other over and over
- Shifting weight back and forth from one leg to the other and rocking
- Happy feet—moving one foot from heel to toe repeatedly
- Tugging on fingers
- Hands active in the front pocket of a hoodie
- Continuous nervous smile or giggle
- Tugging on the end of long sleeves or pulling the hands into the sleeves
- Scratching
- Smoothing hair
- Touching the nose
- Fiddling with eyeglasses
- Rolling and unrolling the note cards
- Mangling the edges of the manuscript
- Trying to flatten the pages of folded speech notes after pulling them out of the pocket at the beginning of the speech
- (Add several that you have observed here)

All of these habits can become so annoying that the audience loses focus on the content. I have watched as students made tally marks to score all the times the speaker continued the annoying patterns. Amazingly, invariably, the speaker had no idea that he was doing whatever it was that all of the audience members noticed. Much more often than not, a classmate will say, "Did you know you kept shifting weight from one foot to the other?" and the speaker will say, "I did?" I have no doubt that if I had asked the principal if he was aware of his constant microphone adjusting, he would say no, too. All of these habits have to be discovered, discussed, and overcome.

Some students decide to solve this issue by making sure they don't do anything distracting. They resolve to stand perfectly, rigidly still. But that still fails the poise test ("easy, self-assured"). The key is to appear calm and confident.

STANCE AND MOVEMENT

Well, then, how should speakers stand? Different people have different styles. For example, I remember my style when I was in college debate tournaments. I always started behind the podium and then moved to the side of it, resting one arm on the podium, crossing one foot over the other, and leaning on the lectern. I would move back to the podium to check my notes and read a quote, and then go to the side again. That worked well for me. Actually, it *still* works for me—if you saw me now giving a keynote speech, you would see that I start at the podium and then move to the side.

Of course, few classrooms have a podium. What works in that case? What do *you* do? You have a favorite delivery position in your classroom, right? That one place where you usually stand when you are in charge? The certain stance you assume? Think about it, and if you can't identify your "home" position, ask your students. They know your style. Similarly, your students will have to discover their own personal positions. Does it work for them to stand with feet shoulder length apart? One foot in front of the other? Do they want to have their arms crossed and comfortable as their base position? One hand in the pocket? Students should test out various poses to see what works for them.

In a classroom without a podium, the speaker is exposed, standing alone at the front of the room, or perhaps with a desk in front of him with note cards on it. Stance and posture become magnified. Most of us find it impossible to stay in one location for the duration of a speech. We have to move to release the nervous energy. The good news is that purposeful motion does not hurt poise. The question is whether the motion is smooth and assured or unnecessary and distracting. Students should never move without a reason for the movement. For example, if they step to the side, they should time the motion to when they are moving from one point to the next in their speech. A couple of steps to one side or the other at transitions can emphasize the organization, the signposts:

Now that I have explained the causes of the war, let's look at the major battles that occurred. (Speaker takes two steps to the left, settles into a good stance.) The Battle of Bull Run was significant because . . . But perhaps the most important battle (Speaker moves back to her original position.) was the Battle of . . .

A step back can indicate that the speaker is done with that part of the speech. A step forward emphasizes an important point. Discuss with students how they can use purposeful movement during a speech, but be sure they know that speakers do have to stand still sometime. Constant motion is distracting.

DEALING WITH MISTAKES

All speakers make mistakes. They forget something; their voices crack; they mispronounce words. Part of poise is learning how to deal with those mistakes.

Teach students not to dwell on a mistake and get off track. They should stay calm, acknowledge the error quickly, and move on. (That's often good advice in other areas, too.) Nervousness tends to wear off as a speech continues. I have watched many students start with shaky hands and unsteady voices yet transform into poised speakers a minute or so into a speech. Making an issue of an early mistake doesn't allow this transition to occur.

A RESPECTFUL CLASSROOM ATMOSPHERE

In truth, not all behaviors can be cured. Many people blush when nervous. You will have students who turn bright red the moment all eyes are on them. Let me talk for a minute, then, about classroom atmosphere. It is extremely important to set up the audience to minimize the discomfort of student speakers. To create a respectful and safe environment for speeches, discuss the difficulty of the task and how uncomfortable it can be to make a speech in front of a group. Reassure students that no one in the room is a professional and experienced speaker. Emphasize the need to be kind and tolerant. We can't laugh at Chloe because she blushes. We can't give Marcus a hard time because his voice cracks.

We have to understand that many speakers will have quivering voices when they start, and we need to be tolerant of that.

This may be a good time to have a discussion of how to be a good listener. Explain the importance of being attentive and quiet, laughing only when appropriate during the speech, avoiding distracting the speaker, responding when the speaker expects a response, and applauding politely when the speaker finishes. The goal is to have the speaker feel that the listeners totally support him as he presents.

EXPERIENCE LEADS TO POISE

So far, I have discussed being aware of all the things speakers do to distract the audience. When your students are aware of their ticks, they can begin to avoid them. But habits are hard to break. Don't expect students (or yourself) to eliminate all annoying behaviors instantly.

A key to developing poise is experience. The more they speak, the better students will be at leaving out the head flicking and shirt tugging. Certainly, it is easier to be poised in familiar situations. The second back-to-school night is not as bad as the first. We need to give students many opportunities to speak in different situations so they can begin to feel comfortable and to develop stage presence.

POSTURE

I cannot leave the poise section without a comment about posture. When I taught an eighth-grade civics lesson, I assigned what I called the Twenty-Eighth Amendment Project. Students had to propose an idea for the next amendment to the Constitution, write a formal research paper, and present a speech to parents who had volunteered to be members of the "Senate committee" conducting a hearing on the proposed amendment. Students were seated during the presentation to the committee, and I was amazed at how they arranged themselves. They slouched in the chair, stretched their legs out in front of the desk, constantly wiggled their feet, and draped one arm over the back of the chair. "Self-possessed assurance of manner" must include presenting yourself in a way that commands respect. Students do not grasp this concept without some help and risk creating bad impressions.

I taught students that when we spoke, we had to become poised first. I am not referring only to that one major presentation. When we had a class discussion, if a student chose to make a comment, she had to get herself ready to make a comment: sit up, avoid annoying habits, and speak. When we conducted traveling debates (see pages 130–131), the speaker had to stand, get settled, and speak. You set up many rules to make your classroom work. It is not at all difficult to set up the expectation that when a student speaks, she has to look composed and sharp, with a posture that shows she's about to present an idea worth listening to.

TIPS FOR BECOMING POISED

With so many possible distracters to poise, it is a good idea to make students aware of a few strategies that can help them calm down. Encourage them to do the following:

1. Visualize. In your mind, go through the entire speech. Visualize the room, the audience, and the place where you will be speaking. Imagine the perfect performance and the audience appreciation. See yourself being successful.
2. Practice. Repeat your performance over and over again. Practice in front of a mirror; practice in front of a friend who will offer constructive criticism; practice in front of the family; practice the speech standing up if you will be standing when you deliver the speech. Ask for feedback about things that indicated lack of poise. (*Typically, students practice until they get the speech right. Suggest that they practice until they cannot get it wrong.*)
3. Take three long, deep breaths before you walk up to speak. Once in place, take one more deep breath. Yes, the audience is watching, but they will allow you to get yourself settled. Don't begin until you feel settled.
4. Acknowledge nervousness by saying something like this: "Please excuse me if my hands tremble. I don't want it to get in the way of the important things I have to say today." Audiences are on your side and are very forgiving.
5. Get a drink and take water up to the podium.
6. Count backward from four very slowly five times before you take

the stage: "Fourrrrrrr, thrrrreeeee, twooooooo, onnnnnnne . . ."
Exhale as you say (or think) each number.

7. Use positive self-talk: "I can do this!" "I am ready!" "They all survived and so will I!"

8. Take a brisk walk before the speech if possible. Go out in the hall five to ten minutes before your speech and get the wiggles out.

PRACTICE IDEAS

1. Ask several students to give two-minute impromptu speeches on topics familiar to them, such as their favorite movie, activity, or sports team. After each speech, ask audience members to discuss what they noticed about the speaker's poise. (I suggest two minutes because most of us can easily talk for thirty seconds, but the true wiggles come out when we start to struggle to keep the speech going.)

2. Model (and have students model) several speech stances. Which stances look comfortable and confident? Which lead to wiggling and fidgeting? Do you have to stay in one place, or can you move smoothly from one location to another?

3. Do any of your students have a Web cam or a computer with a built-in Web camera? Do any have a video camera? Suggest to those students that they video record themselves. Without the pressure of a live audience, some of the ticks may not show up, but it is a good way for students to see themselves as others see them.

[Activities 1, 2, 4, 10, and 15 from Chapter 16 work especially well with this section, but all activities included in that chapter require poise.]

CHAPTER 9:

Voice: Making Every Word Heard

ollowing the PVLEGS mnemonic, voice is the second part of performance that speakers should address. At a minimum, we strive for a voice that is pleasant to hear. Think of the types of voices students are exposed to: the jazz station deejay; the Top 40 station deejay; the infomercial hustler; the president of the United States; other teachers in your school. Some of them have voices you could listen to all day; some have voices that would be too harsh to live with. I don't believe we all need to be as smooth and pleasant as the jazz station deejay, nor do I believe we should encourage students to try to mimic someone else's style. I do believe we need to have students begin to think about how they sound.

A good speech is a good conversation magnified. The speaker retains his basic conversational style but uses animation and volume suitable for a larger audience. Don't encourage students to pretend to be master orators. Have you ever seen a comedian doing a caricature of a southern revival preacher? ("Say yay-ess! I said, say yay-ess!") That is not the goal. Again, you don't want students to imitate any style or any person. You should, however, point out to students that there *are* different types of voices and you should begin the process of having them think about *their* voices. Some people have very strident voices, for example, making it tiring to listen to them. Help students become aware of how they sound to avoid such problems.

VOLUME

Volume is an important part of voice. As a professional speaker, I always check the sound system before a presentation. In the classroom setting the same concern exists. Can everyone comfortably hear what the speaker is saying? Is the volume just right for the space? Does the voice carry to the back corners? Many students speak too softly. Often, a teacher will just repeat a speaker's inaudible comment so the class can hear it. Don't reinforce bad habits. Require the speaker to repeat the comment, and use the occasion to reteach the importance of appropriate volume.

Certainly, before a presentation, we should tell students to consider whether their voices will project to the back of the room. That shy girl who never raises her voice must know that for the four minutes of the speech she has to use a voice bigger than she has ever used in school—the voice she uses when her sister borrows her favorite outfit without asking. Much rarer is the student whose voice is too big for the space. If you have one of those students, rein him in.

ENUNCIATION

The audience needs to be able to hear *every word* of a speech. I emphasize this because often students mumble and/or blur words together. Generally, the volume is fine, but there are moments when enunciation falters, as in these examples:

> *I'mgonnatellyubout the author's life . . .*

> *Knowhudimean? Allovus have felt that way at some point . . .*

> *Jever hear about acid rain? Acid rain is . . .*

"I am going to tell you about" is a seven-word phrase and should not be turned into one word. "Do you know what I mean" may be unnecessary fat (recall the verbal virus section in Chapter 4), but if a student is going to use the phrase, she should say all six words, not one blurred word. "All of us" have heard students make these mistakes, but "did you ever" talk to a class about enunciation? Have you ever stressed the need for each word to be clear and distinct? Make enunciation a routine part of your instruction.

ODD VOCAL PATTERNS

Finally, voice includes odd vocal patterns. Have you ever heard a student whose voice rises at the end of every sentence as if he is continually asking questions?

> *So then he went to the zoo to meet the Pigman? And the Pigman was at the baboon enclosure? And John heard the Pigman calling Bobo? But Bobo wasn't there?*

Many students fade away at the end of a sentence.

> *John went to the zoo to see the Pigman. He found the Pigman feeding peanuts to Bobo.*

I have no idea where these habits come from, but please begin the process of ending them. When they occur, bring them to the student's attention. Discuss how they may diminish the impact of the message. Ask the speaker to repeat the lines without the odd mannerism.

PRACTICE IDEAS

1. Ask students to deliver some short, silly speeches. Project the text of the speech onto a whiteboard or screen, and ask volunteers to step up and speak. (You can download some samples at www.pvlegs.com.) Afterward, ask the class to discuss the voice aspects of the speech. Here is one short speech example:

   There are several things to consider. First, do you feel ready to compete? Second, do you have a game plan you believe in? Third, are you prepared to accept the possibility of defeat? Once you have mentally prepared yourself, only one question should enter your mind: do you want to open with rock, paper, or scissors?

2. Teachers often hold class discussions. Before your class discusses a book, an assignment, or an issue, tell students that in addition to the content of their comments, they should focus on voice. After each student speaks, discuss the substance of the comment. Then, before calling on the next student, make some remarks about the student's volume, enunciation, and vocal pattern. We want students to understand that speaking skills shouldn't only be trotted out for one or two big presentations a year.

3. Many students have computers with podcasting capability. Suggest they make and listen to a podcast using programs such as GarageBand or Audacity. Without a quality microphone the sound can be misleading, but podcasting gives students an idea of how they sound, and it is good practice for enunciation.

4. Computers with newer versions of Windows have an application called Sound Recorder built into the Accessories folder. This application is a simple way for students to record their voices and get an idea of what the listeners' experience will be.

5. Students can use a Web site such as Vocaroo (www.vocaroo.com) to record a talk. The recording can be e-mailed or embedded in a blog, enabling others to give feedback.

[Activities 1, 2, 10, 11, 15, 16, and 17 from Chapter 16 work especially well with this section, but all of the activities included in that chapter involve voice.]

CHAPTER 10:

Life: Putting Passion into the Voice

L istening to students' speeches over the years, I was often re-minded of a time when I took my four-year-old son, Ross, to a school event for his older brother. The principal was droning on and on about something, and, before I could stop him, Ross had put both hands to his mouth, made a loud raspberry sound, and said, "Bor-ring!" As a parent, you are sometimes put into a position of having to tell your child he is wrong, even when he is right.

Similarly, it amazes me how children who are so animated in the lunchroom or at a sleepover can be so flat and dull in the classroom.

We need to hear emotions in students' public presentations: anger, excitement, joy, sadness, fear, disappointment, amazement. Many students believe that adding emotion to their voices will make them decidedly uncool, but it is far less cool to bore your peers to tears. I use the word *life* rather than *inflection* for this element because *life* seems to resonate with students, but use whichever term works for you.

I got a lesson in vocal life many years ago when I had a radio show on a Top 40 station. (It was a talk show called "Rap," to give you an idea of how many years ago it was.) After recording the first show, I listened to the tape. I was boring. I found out that radio and television flatten your voice. To sound normal through the audio speaker, you have to be exceptionally lively in the studio. To a large extent, this is true in public speaking: to sound interesting to the audience, you have to exaggerate the feeling in your voice.

This is a real stretch for many students. They often push back at this point; they worry about sounding foolish in front of their friends when we ask them to animate their voices in a speech. (Oddly, there is no worry when they talk excitedly in the lunchroom.) Without instruction, students tend to be monotonous and remove feeling from their voices.

THE IMPORTANCE OF LIFE IN THE VOICE

Consider these simple phrases:

I don't think you're wrong.

You know you shouldn't do that.

As you read them, did it occur to you that the meaning of the phrases could be changed just by the life you inject into your voice? Can you say the first phrase in a way that seems like you sincerely believe I am not wrong? If you emphasize the words differently, can you say it in a way that makes me sure you believe I *am* wrong? How about, "I don't *think* you are wrong," which suggests that you *know* I am wrong? The second phrase can have multiple meanings, too. How would you say it to suggest that *someone else* was supposed to do that? How would you say it to suggest that I was supposed to have done *something else*? How would you say it to let me know you were angry with me? These are fun exercises that demonstrate the importance of life in the voice.

In a public speaking situation, of course, we are not interested in using emphasis to change meaning but rather to sustain interest and convey the importance of information.

Teach your students the importance of life in the voice and demonstrate how to add life by emphasizing various words and phrases when speaking publicly. Students will generally agree that they have more animated voices in the lunchroom and will insist that this is because the lunchroom chatter is more interesting than, for example, an informational speech on environmental issues. They contend that there is no way to be exciting with or excited by an informational speech: "It's just boring facts." Consider the following speech:

Tropical forests cover just 7 percent of the world's surface, but these forests contain more than half of the world's living species. A sad fact is that these forests are being destroyed. Each year, forty million acres—about the size of the state of Washington—disappear, along with the plants and animals that live there.

When I read that silently to myself, I always "hear" emphasis in my head. I can't read that speech without hearing places where emotion belongs. I suspect I am not alone in this. Certainly, if I were asked to read this aloud, there are places where I would naturally add life: "just *7 percent*" should be said forcefully to emphasize how small the number is, and "contain *more than half*" should be said with amazement, right? But although these inflections are natural to me, they are not natural to students just beginning to develop as speakers.

Some speeches call for modifying the voice to become someone else. Listen to an elementary teacher reading a story. When Eeyore is talking, she changes her voice to become Eeyore. Have you ever overheard students mimicking one of their teachers? Not always flattering, to be sure, but often entertaining. So one way to put life in the presentation is to bring in someone else's life and become that character.

I have had students come show me the text of their speeches and ask for help finding places to add life. I have been amazed that they couldn't see the opportunities. In other words, don't be surprised at how much you need to model. (Yes, there are always one or two students who have drama experience or are gifted performers, but most students need help.) I have great respect for students who work hard trying to put the emotion in the right place. Once when a student asked for help, I highlighted points in her text where I believed emotion was called for. When she performed her speech, she spoke in a monotone except for the parts I'd highlighted (shown here in italics).

The book Stone Fox has an ending that will make you cry. With a small distance to go to the end of the race, the dog's heart burst. Yes, it burst! I was sad and stunned. The remaining teams in the race caught up but stopped instead of passing. The grandson picked up the dead dog and carried the dog across the finish line, pulling the sled behind him. There were tears in the eyes of the spectators. Tears in the eyes! The grandfather looked on . . .

It was an odd effect, to be sure. You may hear speeches like this—speeches that are 95 percent monotonous and 5 percent lively, but that is part of the process. This speech is 5 percent lively now; by the year's end, it will be 20 percent lively. (Were you thinking they could become 100 percent masters in just one year?)

PRACTICE IDEAS

1. Have fun with small phrases. Use phrases like the ones I listed on page 72 and ask students to say them differently to create different meanings. Challenge them to think of ways to alter the delivery of the phrases. "Don't do that to your sister" can be delivered with anger, with the idea that you should have done something else to your sister, with the idea that you should have done it to someone else's sister, or with the idea that you should have done it to your brother. Other phrase ideas can be found at www.pvlegs.com.
2. Have students write a short speech that includes a conversation between two characters. Require a different voice for each character. For example: "My dad said, 'Now, William, stop talking back to me,' which made me reply, 'Well then, I will just shut up. Is that what you want?'" (It is entertaining to hear student versions of what their parents sound like.)
3. Do whole-class choral exercises with fun phrases so that all students can practice inflection together. For example, "Don't ever use my toothbrush on the dog's teeth again!" delivered by an entire class pretending to be angry can be entertaining for students and surprising to teachers in nearby classrooms.
4. Project mini-speeches, such as the tropical forest speech, onto a screen and have student volunteers deliver them. Discuss ways to add life. Ask, *Where can we add feeling? What feeling belongs with this word or phrase?*

[Activities 1, 2, 4, 7, 8, 9, 11, 13, 15, 16, and 17 from Chapter 16 work especially well with this section.]

CHAPTER 11:

Eye Contact: Engaging Each Listener

W hether you are interviewing for a job, talking to a parent at conference time, or speaking in front of a large audience, you have to be mindful of where you are focusing your attention. When I am called in as a consultant to work with a group of students, I do a little demonstration to make clear the power of eye contact. As I begin the discussion, I walk a little closer to some unsuspecting student. I look at him. And I keep looking. Invariably, the student reacts. Perhaps his leg starts jiggling. Maybe he begins to shift a bit in his seat. A nervous smile appears. The student glances up at me and looks away and glances at me and looks away. There may be some squirming. No, I have never had anyone get upset for being put on the spot. I have had a lot of laughs with students, and I have had universal acceptance of the idea that where a speaker looks is very meaningful.

WHERE TO LOOK

Typically, a student giving a speech will look primarily at the teacher. She will look at her notes, then at the teacher, and repeat that process several times. We have done a great job persuading students that we are the people who matter in the classroom. Now we have to convince them that we do not matter more than any other individual in the room. If a student is at the board, overhead projector, or interactive whiteboard demonstrating how to do a problem in math class, he should be looking at the other students. If a student is trying to persuade other students during a class discussion that her argument is the correct one, she should be looking at the students she is trying to persuade. The way to involve listeners is to make eye contact with them.

As teachers, we always look around the room. We know that just glancing over at Julio makes him look up and stop talking. We know that giving Amanda a disapproving stare gets her to stop doodling and refocus. As public speakers, we should always survey the faces in the room as well. The same things happen: listeners look up and focus on us; people who might have been thinking about talking to a neighbor suddenly stop; audience members who were starting to daydream become attentive again. Such is the power of eye contact.

As a speaker I need to look at the audience for two reasons. One, making eye contact ensures that each person feels involved and important. Two, making eye contact gives me feedback about *my* performance. When I was in the classroom, I would occasionally teach a lesson and see my students' confused expressions: "You guys aren't getting this, are you?" I would ask, but I already knew the answer. Their dazed faces cued me right away, but only because I was looking at them.

Students also need to direct their vision toward the *individuals* in the audience. They aren't speaking to a group; they are speaking to many different people. It may seem intimidating to look at each person in the audience, but it is necessary.

Perhaps you have seen studies that have followed the eye contact of teachers. Even the best teachers tend to ignore certain areas of the classroom. Years ago, Adams and Biddle (1970) coined the term "action zone" to describe the area of teacher focus. They discovered that teachers pay more attention to students seated at the front of the class and to those seated down the middle. It takes a conscious effort for most of us to remember the sides and the back corners.

Since it is difficult even for seasoned speakers, it will be very difficult for the beginning speaker to make eye contact with everyone in the audience. We are only beginning the process here. I have seen the student who takes this to heart and *plans* eye contact. In a somewhat robotic fashion, the student glances at his notes, looks at students on the left side of the room, glances at his notes, looks at the students one row in from the left side, and so on, until all of the audience members have been checked off. I applaud that effort. It is a long journey from looking only at notes or staring down to jerking the head up and down and back and forth to smoothly scanning the entire room with a brief connection with the eyes of the audience members.

FAMILIARIZE, DON'T MEMORIZE

A presentation is most powerful if the speaker looks at the audience *constantly*. In a small speech, a class discussion, or an impromptu speech on a familiar topic, this is easier than it is for a major speech. In a longer speech the question becomes this: Should you require students to memorize the big presentation? Is it unfair to demand that they memorize a five-minute speech (750 words, remember) on the topic about which they were supposed to have spent weeks researching? A book they had a month to read? A demonstration they should have practiced many times? If the speech were memorized, constant eye contact would be a lot easier to achieve.

Let's look more closely at the issue of memorization. Recall that I wanted every student to have a complete text of the speech, a word-for-word script, at the end of the building-a-speech process. In some dream world, each student will have read the speech many times before the presentation, rehearsed it out loud, videotaped it, made a podcast, and sat the family down for a couple of dress rehearsals. But that is a world far away from any in which I have taught. It is hardly surprising that some students who give a speech in class have never performed it before that very moment. Memorization by all students is not a realistic expectation.

Total memorization may not be desirable, either. If a student memorizes word for word the entire five- or six-minute speech, two things can happen. One, the speech can sound old and tired. Remember that a good speech is a good conversation magnified. A memorized speech can lose the conversational feel. Two, a small mistake can seem significant if a speaker is working from a memorized speech. If the speaker is thinking word for word, one glitch can throw her off:

The main character in the story, T. S. Spivet, was surprised . . . no, wait . . . wait a minute . . . I mean stunned . . . he was stunned . . .

yes, wait . . . I mean T. S. was stunned when he got the call from the Smithsonian.

The student is so worried about each word that she becomes unable to think of the big picture. It wouldn't have mattered to us as listeners to think of T. S. as surprised rather than stunned. It matters to the word-bound speaker only. Let students know that no speaker delivers a speech exactly the way the text reads.

Don't stress memorization. Stress *familiarization* instead. Theoretically, after all the rehearsals and preparation time, each student is totally familiar with the main ideas. (Back to that dream world . . .) No one should ever use the text when it is performance time. On the other hand, almost no one should try to speak empty-handed. Even the best student may find that the pressure has caused him to go blank temporarily:

My third point is . . . is . . . um, I forgot . . . wait . . . (Nervous smile.) . . .

Choose the middle course. Students should bring note cards or one piece of 8 1/2-by-11-inch paper. In large print or a font easily seen at a glance from three feet away, the main ideas should be listed—triggers, if you will, for the familiar information. Under no circumstances should complete sentences be written on the paper or note card. Perhaps for certain speeches, students can write down facts that can't be memorized or the exact words being quoted. That's all.

Obviously, there is a trick to taking an entire speech text and condensing it to a few key words. I have had success modeling this in two ways. Project on the board the text from some fictional work. Perhaps you can take a passage from a novel the class is currently reading or a passage from a story the students love. Display the entire text. Then, have student volunteers come up and cross out words that can be eliminated, leaving enough key words to make it possible to retell the story. After a few volunteers the significant words remain, and you may get a story that looks like this:

Homer ~~didn't realize that~~ Apu ~~had~~ crossed out ~~the~~ expiration date ~~on the~~ bologna. ~~It was over~~ six months past the time ~~the product should have been taken off of the shelf. Unknowing,~~ Homer ate the entire pack ~~even though he started to feel sick. You know Homer, — he just had to finish. Homer~~ ended up so sick ~~that an~~ ambulance ~~had to be called and he was~~ rushed to the hospital. Apu ~~became~~ remorseful and ~~decided to do something to~~ make amends.

Once students have the concept, take the text of one student's speech and go through the same process. Project the entire script and have students whittle away at it. Ultimately, you will get something workable for a note card to use during the speech.

Before:

The study of angiogenesis has two exciting potential applications for dealing with significant health issues in America. First, we may find a way to inhibit the growth of cancerous tumors. Those tumors depend on adequate blood supply and the growth of new blood vessels (angiogenesis). If we can find a way to inhibit angiogenesis, we can cut off the supply of blood and nutrients to the tumors. Second, we may find a way to limit obesity. Fat cells also require blood supplies and antiangiogenesis drugs and foods may be part of an answer to our obesity epidemic.

After:

ANGIO: 2 APPLICATIONS HEALTH
1. CANCER—CUT BLOOD SUPPLY TO TUMORS
2. OBESITY—FAT CELLS REQUIRE BLOOD

Then, do the process in reverse. Hand each student one note card. Challenge them to put key words on the note cards as you speak, with the goal of being able to retell your story using the note card. Use a speech like the one about tropical forests on page 73 in Chapter 10. Students as young as fourth graders have been successful turning that speech into a note card like this:

Trop forests
7% of world
½ of species
each year size of Wash. destroyed and plants/animals

And what does all this have to do with eye contact? You have seen the student who has a fistful of note cards and loses her place, right? The solution? Don't allow a fistful of note cards. As I said, a presentation is most powerful if the speaker is constantly looking at the members of the audience. In a two-minute speech about a student's favorite activity, that is easy to pull off. In a seven-minute speech about Afghanistan for world geography class, it is not so easy. Having brief phrases on one or two note cards removes the possibility that the speaker will read to us and never look up. Having only major headings on the note card makes it easy for the speaker to glance down quickly and then resume eye contact.

Using notes effectively is tricky. It takes practice. It is easier, though, when students have the right tool in front of them. The complete text stapled in the corner? No. The entire script cut into pieces and pasted on note cards? No. Two note cards with several bullet points or trigger words on each? Yes.

PRACTICE IDEAS

1. Let student volunteers speak for one minute about a topic they love (favorite sports team, store, class, grandparent, etc.). At the end of each speech, ask students in the audience to raise their hands if they thought the speaker looked at them at some point during the speech. This creates a great visual of where the student was focusing as he or she spoke.
2. Project a small speech on the board. Something silly, like this one, will do:

   Class, there are three reasons why crunchy peanut butter is better than creamy peanut butter. First, crunchy peanut butter has texture. We aren't babies eating mashed baby food anymore!

Second, crunchy peanut butter is mature. Studies have shown that adults over twenty-one prefer crunchy by 46 percent. Finally, crunchy peanut butter has little bits that get stuck in your braces or between your teeth. You can have fun later during class trying to get the stuck pieces out with your tongue.

Tell the class to turn away from the board and face the back of the room. Then ask a student volunteer speaker to stand at the back of the room, facing the class and the board where the speech is projected. The volunteer speaker can practice glancing up at the screen and back down at the faces as he or she delivers the speech.

[Activities 1, 2, 3, 4, 10, 14, and 16 from Chapter 16 work well with this section.]

CHAPTER 12:

Gestures: Matching Motions to Words

Watch people in some public place as they converse. Look around a restaurant or coffee shop. Sit on a bench in the mall and watch people walking by. Sneak a peek at friends a few seats over on the bus. Odds are that as they speak, they are gesturing. Hands move, faces emote, and body positions change. This is typical and natural. Sure, some people use gestures more than others, but it seems that when humans talk, the body moves.

Watch your students in the lunchroom. Along with the animation you hear in their voices, you can see the animation in their hands and faces. When they are loose and relaxed, they gesture.

We gesture all the time without thinking about it. When I work with classes, I often ask students to be aware of *my* gestures. When you ask students to pay attention to gestures, it is quite entertaining. Here's how the experience usually goes when I demonstrate:

MY GESTURE: *Holding up the right hand with palm out.*

MY WORDS: Wait. Stop for a minute and pay attention to my gestures. See? There's one. I just made a stop gesture with my right hand.

MY GESTURE: *Holding up the left hand with one finger extended, pointing at the right hand.*

MY WORDS: This is my "wait/stop" gesture. I held up a hand with the palm out. Did you notice? And wait a second. Check this out. See my left hand? I have one finger pointed at the "wait" gesture. This is my "did-you-notice-my-gesture?" gesture.

MY GESTURE: *The right hand and left hand now point at each other.*

MY WORDS: And wait a minute. There was another gesture. See how my right finger is now pointed at my left finger that was pointing at the "wait" gesture? This is getting confusing, isn't it? My right hand changed from the wait/stop gesture to the pointing gesture. Crazy, huh?

The class focuses on every move now, and because I tend to have very expressive hands, the chain of gestures gets quite long. With this beginning, we discuss the way gestures improve speaking and engage listeners.

We also discuss the randomness of gestures. By this, I mean that the way *I* indicate "wait" might be quite different than the way *you* indicate "wait." My gesture for describing a terrible-tasting food is probably different from yours. If you ask three people to come up with a gesture for a heart that is beating really fast, you will probably get three slightly different motions. That's fine. There is not a right and wrong to gestures, for the most part. That is part of the fun of gestures.

You would think that all the animated behavior in the hallway and lunchroom would transfer to the classroom and the presentation, but it often doesn't. On stage, the free-flowing gestures stop, partly due to tension from nervousness, partly due to fear of embarrassment. But without gestures, a speech is incomplete.

Gestures support words. If you say, "There are three reasons . . ." and hold up three fingers, the audience has gotten your message in two modes. Gestures add drama. If you want to describe how mad you were when the teacher gave you a bad grade, a good facial expression will help. Gestures involve the audience. If you ask, "How many of you love pizza?" and raise your hand to model, listeners respond. Gestures add emphasis. A clenched fist pounding on the palm of the hand definitely emphasizes how upset you are at the new dress code. Gestures also can help you get rid of nervous energy. You don't have to be still and let us see how shaky your hands are.

Some speeches have gestures built in. Recall once again the brown bag speech. Obviously, some motions are implied in that speech: reach into the bag, pull out the mini soccer ball, hold it up for the class to see, and so on. But haven't you seen students who do a poor job of that? Maybe they don't hold the ball high enough for everyone to see, or maybe they don't show the picture long enough or don't show it to all sides of the room. How are students supposed to learn those things?

Why not give them a list of ideas?

- When counting, hold up fingers. Say, "First . . ." while holding up one finger; "Second . . ." while holding up two fingers, and so on.
- Use descriptive gestures. When describing size, use your hands: if you say, "It was about two feet long . . . ," hold your hands about two feet apart with the palms facing each other. If you say, "The dog was about three feet tall . . . ," hold one hand three feet above the floor. Use hands to draw the words: if you say, "He rode the waves of the ocean," move your hand up and down; if you say, "His hat had a triangular shape," trace the shape in the air with your pointer finger.
- Use emphatic gestures. "And suddenly (*slap hands together*), they were gone!" "We cannot (*pound on the table*) allow this!" Clench your fists to indicate anger.
- Match your face to your mood. Smile when telling a funny story; open your eyes wide when talking about a surprise; furrow your brow when describing something upsetting; make a face when talking about that bad smell in science class.
- Use hands to control the audience. Say, "Raise your hand if you think . . ." while raising your hand. Say, "Look at this poster . . ." while pointing at the poster.
- Use your shoulders. Say, "I don't know . . ." while shrugging.
- Move your head. Shake your head "no" while saying, "Was putting pickles on my peanut butter sandwich a good idea?" (at least I think you would be shaking your head "no"!).
- Move your body. Say, "Do you want to know a secret?" while leaning toward the audience. Say, "No way" while rocking back away from the audience.

- Use your eyes. If you say, "Way off in the distance," squint and look over the heads of the audience into the "distance."

And this list is only the beginning. When you have your class focus on gestures, they will add things they notice.

BODY TALK

Most people think that gestures only refer to hand motions. As the previous list indicates, facial gestures can be equally powerful. You often adjust a lesson based solely on the quizzical looks on your students' faces. You probably recognize when your spouse is angry before a word has been spoken. But you may have overlooked this: facial gestures not only convey messages, they also have the power to change the face of the person listening. I watched my wife read aloud to her fourth-grade class. At one point in the book *Matthew's Meadow*, the character blows the seeds of a milkweed pod into the breeze. As my wife pursed her lips, half of the class pursed their lips as well. We mimic what we see. If you walk into your class with a huge grin, I guarantee a large number of students will start smiling.

I'm sure you have seen a storyteller who used great body motions to enhance his story. Maybe he hunched over to become the evil witch or stood tall to be the giant. Body gestures are effective in other situations, too. If I take a step back and turn my shoulders slightly, don't you get the idea that I don't want to hold the tarantula you brought in for science class? If I take a step toward a student and lean over her desk, doesn't she get the idea that she should get back to work? What would you do with your body to indicate that you thought an idea suggested to you was ridiculous?

I have had students with very expressive faces but fairly quiet hands, students with very active hands and little body language, and so on. Each student has a style, and so do you. As speakers become more relaxed and more confident, the style shows up, and the gestures begin to flow. Be aware that it can be a long journey from clutching the podium or having a death grip on the note cards to smooth, well-timed gestures. The beginning speaker may be formulaic, and some students actually write gesture directions into their scripts:

*There are three reasons for this. (Pause. Raise three fingers. Pause.)
First, not everyone believes global warming exists. I don't know
why. (Pause. Shrug. Pause).*

I applaud that effort. This student has the idea. This year, 5 percent
smooth, next year . . .

As a final note, remember that gestures are only possible if you have
worked on a couple of prerequisites. Remember the admonition about
the need for familiarization with the script? It is impossible to use a full
range of gestures if you are holding note cards or a sheaf of papers. Tell
your students to put the notes down. Remember the discussion about
poise? Ask them to take their wiggling hands out of the front pocket
of their hoodies and to stop twirling the strands of hair at the side of
their faces. Now they can gesture.

PRACTICE IDEAS

1. Ask students to keep track of *your* gestures in a normal class. As
   you explain a typical assignment, let them focus on all the motions you make.
2. Give students an opportunity to give a one- or two-minute
   speech about a familiar topic. Let the class discuss the gestures
   they saw and/or suggest gestures that would have worked in
   the speech.
3. Enlist the support of an animated student. Have this student
   deliver a speech *without* gestures. Make sure he includes some
   exciting event in the speech, such as describing the time his sister
   wrecked his bicycle or his brother fell down the stairs.
4. Give students a fun homework assignment. Their mission: to get
   a family member to mimic their facial expression. For example,
   tell students to go up to Dad and say, "Dad! Guess what?" with a
   big, happy face with eyebrows up. Dad will look back with raised
   eyebrows and say, "What?" Or, have them try going up to Mom
   with a furrowed brow and saying, "Mom, I have a problem."

Mom will furrow her brow too.

5. Videotape a speech and play it back without sound. Discuss the gestures, body language, and facial expressions the speaker used. What movements seem unintentional? What gestures could the speaker have added? How would the effect of the speech be different with or without these movements? (You have already suggested that every student who can videotape his or her presentation do so before the day of the in-class speech, right? Encourage these students to play their own tapes without sound to see how they look.)

6. Put on the board some phrases or speeches that demand many gestures, such as those in the following list. More examples like these can be found at www.pvlegs.com.

This affects *everyone!*

We have to *stop right now!*

The bucyrus valve is a *tiny, tiny* part of the vivofletzer.

They were *huge*—bigger than a car, even bigger than a house. Suddenly, there were *three* more of them. My *heart started beating so fast* I thought it was going to *burst.* I *looked around* for a place to hide. The killer hamburgers were after me.

[Activities 1, 2, 11, 14, and 16 from Chapter 16 work well with this section.]

CHAPTER 13:

Speed: Pacing for a Powerful Performance

W hat is the most common comment teachers make when a student gives a presentation? My guess is, "Slow down!" Excitement, nerves, and the adrenaline rush of showtime lead to increased speed. Your students are not lying when they say, "I *know* it was five minutes long when I practiced last night!" after you tell them that the speech lasted three minutes and forty-seven seconds. Giving a speech in front of Mom in the living room is not the same as presenting it to thirty peers in the classroom. We *know* this, but do we prepare students for this? Do we give them a warning *before* the speech to expect this problem? Not often enough, if at all. So, to begin with, we should discuss with students the need to pay attention to the speed of the delivery. Then, we can teach them the more complex issues of pacing and using pauses.

SPEED

Think back to the lesson on poise. A student who has practiced will have a smaller problem with nerves and will be less likely to rush. A student who used calming techniques will control the adrenaline better than the student who ignored those tips. But even those students will talk faster than normal. I have given many, many speeches, and I am willing to bet that even now I say more words per minute on stage than I do in rehearsal. Again, with more speaking opportunities comes more control, so give students many opportunities to practice.

The speed of delivery affects the enunciation and the audience's ability to hear *every* word. Did you say, "We need tee liminate"? Because that is what the audience heard when the phrase "We need to eliminate" was rushed through. An overly fast delivery has another major problem, too. The audience gets tired. The listeners' ears wear out. I know that doesn't sound possible, but it is true. A speaker can lose the audience quickly if they have to exert too much effort listening to what is being said.

PACING

There is a more sophisticated aspect to speed, though. It is not just about talking too fast or not; it is about using the speed of delivery—pacing—to enhance the message. This is too much for the novice to comprehend. I don't recommend spending a lot of time teaching pacing until students have gotten comfortable with all the other parts of speaking. But I will tell *you* about it.

You probably adjust the pace of your words without thinking about it. If you are describing the person who was painfully slow in front of you at the ATM machine, you probably slow down your story:

He punched in one number . . . then another number . . . then another number . . . then he waited . . . and finally punched in another number . . .

If you are describing the kickoff return for a touchdown, you probably speed up:

He caught it at the five and before you could blink, he was at the fifteentwentytwentyfive and thengone.

I would be surprised if you said it this way:

He caught it at the five . . . before you could blink . . . he was at the fifteen . . . the twenty . . . the twenty five . . . and then g . . . o . . . n . . . e."

For dramatic effect, the pace should match the words. We should speed up a little for an exciting part or when describing something fast. We should slow down when the mood gets serious or sad or when we're describing something slow. This may come naturally to experienced teachers who still read aloud with the class.

We also need to adjust the pace for emphasis. Think about the huge difference in impact between these two statements:

You . . . must . . . do . . . something . . . now!
You must do something now!

If a parent says, "Don't. You. Ever. Ever. Do. That. Again," odds are the kid won't ever do that again. There is power in slowing down.

PAUSING

Few speakers master it, but pausing is powerful. This was reinforced for me when I spoke at my son's wedding. I thought the father of the bride was required to speak, not the father of the groom, but I guess the wedding couple wanted to break with tradition. I have given hundreds of speeches and led countless seminars and trainings, but I had never given a wedding speech for my son. You can rehearse the words, but you can't rehearse the emotions. I got choked up. I said, "When Greg was little . . ." and stopped. I stood there holding up one finger to indicate "just give me a minute" and waited to gather myself. And because I am a student of speaking, I also noticed that I totally owned that room. Every eye was riveted on me. No one made a sound. For thirty seconds not one person did a thing except give me undivided attention. As a rhetorical technique, it was awesome, though it was not by design. One pause, one gesture, complete power over the audience. I did not decide to create a dramatic effect, but a pause created a dramatic effect nonetheless. A pause is a bold move. Coming to a complete stop? Scary. But very powerful.

Sometimes a brief pause helps a point sink in:

There are three reasons. Three. (Pause.) This is the most important . . .

Four hundred thousand deaths a year from smoking. Four hundred thousand. (Pause.)

A pause is useful after a rhetorical question:

What would you do? (Pause.) I know. It's tricky, isn't it? (Pause.) Did you get that? (Pause.) Four hundred thousand. (Pause.)

Stopping adds drama:

Bullying in our school has to stop now. Right now. (Pause by mentally counting one one thousand, two one thousand, three one thousand, four one thousand.) Each of you must take a stand.

It is hard to muster up enough courage to stand in front of an audience in silence for four seconds. It is hard for you to be still and allow four seconds of wait time after asking a question to the class, isn't it? So you can understand why it is almost impossible for students. But that doesn't mean we can't make them aware of the possibilities.

PRACTICE IDEAS

1. Work on the speed of delivery of simple speeches written with obvious places for speeding up and slowing down. Project them on the screen or give students a handout such as the following. (More ideas are at www.pvlegs.com.)

   Life is too crazy. We are always busy. We rush to get up, wolf down breakfast, run to school, race to practice, hustle through homework, do our chores. We are always in a hurry. What if one day we just stopped? I mean stopped. Dead halt. Catch your breath. Relax. Take a break. It will improve your life.

2. Time students delivering the same speech at different paces. How fast can someone read it with each word distinct? Notice what happens at high speed. Try this from *Star Trek*:

Space: the final frontier. These are the voyages of the starship *Enterprise*. Its continuing mission: to explore strange new worlds, to seek out new life and new civilizations, to boldly go where no one has gone before.

3. Ask student volunteers to read a section from a textbook at slow, medium, and fast speeds. Which is most effective for understanding the text? Try other kinds of text.
4. Take famous speeches from books, plays, and movies to use for practicing. Here is an example from *Shoeless Joe*:

They'll turn up your driveway, not knowing for sure why they're doing it, and arrive at your door, innocent as children . . .

"Of course, we won't mind if you look around," you'll say. "It's only twenty dollars per person." And they'll pass over the money without even looking at it—for it is money they have and peace they lack.

They'll walk out to the bleachers and sit in shirtsleeves in the perfect evening, or they'll find they have reserved seats somewhere in the grandstand or along one of the baselines—wherever they sat when they were children and cheered their heroes, in whatever park it was, whatever leaf-shaded town in Maine, or Ohio, or California. They'll watch the game, and it will be as if they have knelt in front of a faith healer or dipped themselves in magic waters . . .

I don't have to tell you that the one constant through all the years has been baseball. America has been erased like a blackboard, only to be rebuilt and then erased again. But baseball has marked time while America has rolled by like a procession of steamrollers. (Kinsella 1982, 212–213)

Ask students: Where would a pause be effective? Where would you speed up or slow down?

[Activities 1, 2, 15, and 16 from Chapter 16 work well with this section.]

PART IV
PUTTING THEORY INTO PRACTICE

Whew. That is a lot to think about and a daunting amount to teach. Building a speech has five parts; performing a speech has six more parts. That's eleven things I have to add to my already overcrowded curriculum. How can that be done?

First, let's step back and look at the big picture. If I told you that you had to teach writing, including content, organization, word choice, voice, sentence structure, paragraphing, spelling, punctuation, and capitalization, what would you do? If I told you that you had to teach math, including addition, subtraction, multiplication, division, adding and subtracting fractions, multiplying and dividing decimals, the formulas for area, perimeter, and volume of a cylinder, what would you do? What *do* you do? One thing you *don't* do is to assume that you have to teach all of that by yourself today. You work bit by bit, and you build on what others have done before you. If we create a common language for the school or district, teaching speaking becomes a shared responsibility. You won't have to start from scratch.

In addition, you shouldn't "do" speaking as a unit and then move on to the poetry unit or the skeletal system unit or the trappers and traders unit. Speaking can be part of *every* unit and *every* subject. Of the hundreds of teachers I have worked with, I have never met one who didn't have speaking activities already built into the curriculum, no matter what subject they taught. Every one of them had discussions, sharing, answering questions, explaining solutions to problems at the board, presenting projects or book reports, reading aloud, telling stories, participating in mock trials, explaining science experiments, and many, many more speaking opportunities. Some of these activities were informal, and some were more formal. Some were part of everyday instruction and routines, and some were special events with special audiences, including grandparents, parents, and community members. You don't teach speaking in isolation; you teach it in the context of all of those activities. The biggest difference is that *before* you read this book, there may have been little or no focused teaching of speaking skills prior to those activities. Now that will change. To some extent, then, nothing new has been added to the curriculum. We'll just teach what we were teaching, but better, more purposefully, and more specifically.

CHAPTER 14:

Every Day Through the End of the Year

I have never been a fan of teaching skills in isolation, no matter what the skill. I never handed out a worksheet about word choice unless something made a word choice lesson necessary and relevant. Perhaps some novel had unique language—a good time to talk about word choice. A lesson on political parties is not effective without tying it in to a current event, such as the debate on immigration, where students can observe party differences in action. Learning about .com, .gov, and .edu is important knowledge to have in order to be Internet savvy, but why teach this information unless you are going to assign some research project that sends students to the Internet?

Let me make two suggestions, then. Suggestion one is to teach speaking skills when you introduce the *special* speaking assignment, that one *big show*. Maybe you have assigned a big book report project. Perhaps you have given students a month to read a novel and prepare an oral presentation in which they dress up as a character from that novel. Maybe, at the end of your poetry unit, you plan to have a poetry café in which students share their poems and adults are invited for tea and cookies. That kind of thing. In my case, when I taught civics, it was the Supreme Court project, as you may have guessed. During this study of the judicial branch, I gave each student the name of a significant Supreme Court case—a case that changed America. I asked them to research the case, understand its significance, and be able to explain how it affects us today. I told them they would present the case to the class and to invited guests (generally, parents and grandparents who could get off work, and occasionally administrators whom I talked into coming by). Because the Supreme Court is formal, students had to dress up on the day they presented. Students had one month to prepare the five- to six-minute speech. That was not a suggested time frame. The speech had to be between five and six minutes long (nothing less than five minutes would be scored; at six minutes they would be forced to stop). As you can see, I set this up to be a big deal indeed. Situations like these would be good times to teach students how to do an oral presentation.

Suggestion two is to teach speaking skills at the beginning of the year when you set up class procedures. Maybe you don't have a special presentation until the end of the year. For example, I have worked with schools that have an annual tradition. The entire year builds to some big culminating activity, and exit projects are required. If you teach speaking skills at that time, you miss the benefit of improved communication all year. The students will benefit and carry the skills with them so discussions and speeches in next year's classes will be better, but from August through May this year, *your class* missed out. You want improved speaking in your classroom all year.

Maybe you don't have any *special* presentation at all during the year but just want better oral communication during routine classroom business—discussions, solving problems at the board, responding to questions, working with partners, and so on. In this case also, early in the year when you set up class procedures, set up speaking procedures: "This is how we turn in papers; this is how we keep the assignment book; this is how we use hall passes; this is how we speak. Final papers must be in ink or word-processed; comments in class require poise and voice." This is not difficult to set up. Make it known early in the year that speaking matters, and teach students all that is involved even in less formal public speaking.

TEACH THE PROCEDURES

Here is how I teach speaking skills. I take two class periods of about fifty minutes each. For schools on a block plan, this is a one-day lesson; for others, two consecutive days are required. If we are talking about the *big show* scenario, I recommend this training after the introduction of the project. In that case, on day one, explain the big project and give the big picture of where students are headed. Hand out the project requirements, the rubric, useful materials—the kinds of things you give students when you make the big assignment. On days two and three, teach speaking skills. (Remember, this assumes that none of the teachers in your school has this book and no one has introduced this before. When I was teaching, that was certainly the case, and it has been true in my consulting as well.)

If you aren't building to the big presentation, block out two periods early in the year when you are setting up class norms. Perhaps you are planning to have weekly discussions about current events. After the first discussion, suggest to students that discussions could be better. Take two days to show them how. The bottom line: starting from nothing, teaching all the skills really can be done in two class periods.

Here is what you should do in those two periods. During the first period devoted to teaching speaking, explain the two parts of speaking (building a speech and performing a speech) and help students clarify these parts in their minds. Then teach the elements of building a speech. In truth, this part is pretty dry: use lecture and explanation, PowerPoint slides, bullet points, the SMART Board. Not the most exciting class, but a very important one. You can explain building a speech in forty minutes. Then, for the last ten or so minutes of the period, introduce the teaser. Read the part of this book about the importance of performance on pages 55–56. Tell students that you will introduce them to PVLEGS, a guaranteed way to become a great speaker. Set up the students for participation and laughter. Stress the need for students to be able to laugh at themselves—that we *will* laugh as we play with performances.

The second class period is all about performing a speech. There are two ways to conduct this class: using student volunteers and using illustrative video clips. I prefer the first way because I have used this method for a long time. It worked with students in my own classes, and it works when I coach a class as a consultant. If you don't feel comfortable trying it, go with video clips.

Generally I ask for student volunteers to deliver a speech, and I observe and comment on the speech, focusing on the skill that is going to be introduced next. Then I introduce the skill. I believe that for maximum effect, student volunteers work best.

TEACHER: I need a volunteer who is brave and willing to laugh at himself or herself. Yes, we might laugh. We are going to play and have fun and begin to become good performers, but because we are not all experts yet, some silly things will happen. Sometimes we will look funny or sound funny. There is always awkwardness learning something new. You can probably ride a bicycle well now, but your first ride without training wheels was humorous. So I need volunteers who realize that we aren't expecting anything other than trying; volunteers who want to learn and are willing to look like they did the first time without training wheels. But the good part is that you will learn something important about your mistakes so you can avoid them when the real performance happens. Wouldn't you rather discover the mistakes now instead of the day of the big show? Any volunteers?

BRANDON: Okay.

TEACHER: Good! Come up to the front of the room here. Tell us about a favorite activity of yours, whatever it is that you know a lot about and love doing, okay?

BRANDON: Okay. (*Nervous smile.*) Um. (*Tugging at shirt tail.*), I love playing Grand Theft Auto (*Still tugging at shirt tail.*). And I like it 'cuz it has lots of action and crashes and, you know, like, action (*Pause, nervous smile, wiggling.*). What else am I supposed to say? (*Tugging at shirt.*)? Oh, I know. And the graphics are really cool, and I like driving fast.

Depending on the kind of teacher you are and the relationship you have with your class, you have a couple of options here. I am a performer, and I like to play with the kids. I take the position the student was in and copy the speech, exaggerating the behaviors. I mimic his actions. I readily admit that few teachers will be bold enough to be on stage like this, but if you are brave, and if the kids trust you to make gentle fun of them, the students will love the demonstration and really get the idea that some behaviors are problematic. If you set up the activity well and prequalify the volunteers, this can be memorable and a lot of fun. If you are not comfortable with what may be an over-the-top idea, simply discussing the behaviors you and the class noticed will be effective.

CREATE A SAFE SPACE FOR SPEAKING UP

It is important to set up the rules for a discussion and critique of a student sample speech. Harkening back to my comments in Chapter 8 about creating a respectful atmosphere, give students some ground rules. We have to separate the actor from the action: the action may be less than acceptable, but the actor should never be made to feel that *he or she* is less than acceptable. Explain to students that comments can be made on the performance, but not on the person. Comments must simply state the facts: "He tugged at his shirt"; "She shifted weight from one leg to the other"; "He never looked up from his notes." Explain that constructive comments are helpful, and give a few examples: "I think she could have more feeling when she talks about finding the money"; "He should show with his hands how large the animal was." Finally, let students know that positive comments are appreciated: "His facial expressions were really cool"; "She started out looking nervous but did a great job calming down." Here's how a discussion of Brandon's impromptu speech might go:

> **TEACHER:** Let's talk about Brandon's speech, not the words, though. What did you notice about his actions?
>
> **CLASSMATE:** Well, he tugged at his shirt a lot.
>
> **CLASSMATE:** He kept smiling and kinda laughing.

Take another volunteer and give the same assignment.

> **ARMIDA:** (*Smiling.*) I love shopping and hanging out at the mall. (*Head flip to get hair out of eyes.*) Me and my friends go every weekend. (*Head flip to get hair out of eyes.*) We look at shoes a

lot. (*Head flip to get hair out of eyes.*) Oh, and we check out guys. (*Laughing, head flip to get hair out of eyes.*)

TEACHER: What did you notice about Armida?

You can see how this works. After the discussion, introduce the skill you want students to work on.

TEACHER: The first part of performing a speech is poise. Without poise, listeners will not be able to pay attention to the speech. (*Share the ideas and information from the poise section of this book in Chapter 8, and show the list of problem behaviors on page 61.*) Does someone want to volunteer to give a speech with poise?

Almost certainly the next volunteer will be more poised than Brandon and Armida. That is how fast students pick up on the skill. They haven't mastered poise, of course, but they have the concept, and they know what to look for. They will be watching speakers with a new awareness and a critical eye. They will be evaluating every speaker they see from now on, including you. All you need to do is reinforce this process as the year goes on, as I will explain later.

Introduce the remaining skills (voice, life, eye contact, gestures, and speed) in the same manner. First, ask another student to volunteer to deliver a speech. Then, invite feedback and steer the discussion toward the next skill you want students to learn. In the following example, we use a scripted speech instead of an impromptu speech and we move on from discussing poise to discussing voice.

TEACHER: Now, who would like to volunteer to read the speech I have on the screen?

PAYAM: (*Standing up to read the speech.*) There are several things to consider. First, do you feel ready to compete? Second, do you have a game plan you believe in? Third, are you prepared to accept the possibility of defeat? Once you have mentally prepared yourself, only one question should enter your mind: do you want to open with rock, paper, or scissors?

TEACHER: Any comments?

CLASSMATE: He had good posture and stance, but he tugged at his fingers sometimes.

TEACHER: True, but what if I told you that I don't want to talk about poise right now? What if I asked you a different question: How many of you heard every word Payam said?

(*Only a few hands go up.*)

Explain.

CLASSMATE: He wasn't loud enough for me to hear back here.

CLASSMATE: I heard most of what he said but I missed some.

TEACHER: Very good. Now Payam knows one thing to focus on before the presentations next month. Let's take another volunteer.

REBECCA: There are sevral things to consider. First, dyew feel ready . . . (*Finishes the speech speaking quickly, without enunciating words clearly.*)

TEACHER: Could you hear every word? Was every word clearly spoken? (*Discussion follows.*) The second part of performance is voice. (*Share the ideas and information from the voice section in Chapter 9.*)

And so on. I have found this to be an engaging and effective way to introduce PVLEGS and to teach the skills to students. Invariably, students will make exactly the mistakes I hoped for. But if you have a student who surprises you with great life in her voice, for instance, that's fine, too. Use it as an example of where you want all the students to be, to supplement the examples of mistakes to avoid. You win either way. At the end of the day students know the skills that make up a great presentation. They will not master PVLEGS in one day, but the concepts will be indelibly etched into their minds.

OTHER METHODS

Though I have never had one problem in all the years I have conducted classes this way, I realize that some teachers may feel it is inappropriate to put students on the hot seat like this. What I recommend in that case is to build a file of video clips. Explanation alone will not suffice. *Seeing* and *hearing* is much more powerful. If you choose this method of introducing the concepts, show a demonstrative video clip or two of a poise problem and then discuss it. Then, show a clip of a voice problem and discuss it, and so on.

How do you get the video clips? One option is to have student volunteers act in a movie. Use an inexpensive video camera to record the performance. Your student actors can demonstrate the behaviors I mentioned previously: tugging at the shirt, twirling hair, and so on. Another option is to look for video clips online. Of course, most people in the media are chosen because they *have* PVLEGS and don't make mistakes, but you can find examples. Maybe an actor in a TV show or film is playing a character who is awkward. Possibly an otherwise polished performer or politician has an odd habit. People interviewed on TV news programs and contestants on game shows may demonstrate problems you want to highlight.

Why focus on the problems and not show examples of polished performers? In my experience, students are aware that some people are great performers, but they do not know about all the things that can diminish a performance. They certainly aren't aware of some of the things *they* do, as my children's principal wasn't aware of his microphone fidgeting. Showing them the pitfalls encourages them to look for—and then avoid—those pitfalls in their own performances.

No matter how you present the information on day two, you will have invested two hours of class time presenting the elements of oral communication. That is only the beginning. During the rest of the year, you need to allow time for maintenance and reinforcement. One way to do that is to make references each time you ask students to speak in class. Before a class discussion, it takes very little time to say, "Let's focus on poise today. Before you speak, think about how you present yourself." After the discussion, take a couple of minutes to talk about the speaking skill of the day. Ask, "What did you notice about poise in today's discussion? Who impressed you? Why? Did you see some distracting habits? Which ones?" Before the students give their weekly current events reports, it is not burdensome to say, "Pay attention to life in your voices today. Make the news come alive for us." Spend two or three minutes afterward discussing life in the voice. If you do these things, you will be amazed at your students' growth in oral communication skills. Discussions in June will not be like discussions in September.

Another way to continue development of oral communication is through mini-lessons. When I taught English, I noticed common errors in the assignments I received. If I noticed that students seemed to be having a problem with correct comma usage, for instance, I interrupted my big plan to offer a small lesson about commas. In the same manner, maybe you notice that verbal viruses have infected your students as they answer questions in class. Stop for a few minutes and use an activity from the "Discussion Ideas" in Chapter 4 (pages 32–33) to remind students to avoid verbal viruses. Before storytelling presentations, insert a few mini-lessons about gestures; before persuasive speeches, present some mini-lessons about life. Students need to know that improving speaking skills will require continual effort.

Yes, teaching speaking will take time from some other activities in your curriculum. Not as much as you think, perhaps, but some time nonetheless: two days to set the stage, a couple of minutes every time you have a speaking activity to make it more purposeful, pieces of a few class periods for mini-lessons, and a couple of extra minutes after each student's big presentation so class members can express their reactions, as I will explain in Chapter 15. Don't think of this as borrowed time but rather as value added. As I mentioned at the beginning of this book, your students will thank you for improving their speaking ability.

CHAPTER 15:
Evaluating Speeches

For most speeches you will have two kinds of evaluation: instant feedback from the audience and written feedback from you, the teacher.

In the past you might have run class presentations like this: one student would march up to the front of the classroom and give his speech. As he was speaking, you filled out the score sheet. When he finished, the rest of the class applauded. (I encourage you to insist on applause to acknowledge the speaker, no matter what kind of performance.) The first student sat down, and the next got up.

Notice which person matters in this scenario? The teacher who filled out the score sheet. The teacher shouldn't be the only audience member speakers need to worry about. The speech should be for the class and scored by the class. I use a simple 1 to 5 scale, with 5 being excellent and 1 representing no effort at all. At the end of the speech I ask for a show of hands for each part of PVLEGS:

For poise, how many of you give Tom a 5? (Two hands go up.) A 4? (Nineteen hands go up.) A 3? (Five hands go up.) Hmm, looks like a 4. For voice, how many give Tom a 5? (One hand.) A 4? (Four hands.) A 3? (Twenty-three hands.) Okay, a 3. Let's score life. Five? (Zero hands.) Four? (Zero hands.) Three? (Five hands.) Two? (Twenty-five hands.) Okay, looks like a two.

When I was teaching I made those scores a part of the actual grade. Yes, *my* scoring was worth more, but the student speaker was able to get instant feedback from a real audience. Tom knew that poise was one of his strengths. He discovered that life was a weak spot and something to focus on next time.

I know some readers may object to having students grade each other. Let me try to anticipate and address some of the concerns:

- "Student grading turns the speech into a popularity contest." Not true. Give students more credit than that. I have never been disappointed in the results of peers evaluating peers. Students who have learned the criteria absolutely know a poised speaker when they see one. Yes, Martin may be your best friend, but won't you feel foolish when your hand is the only one raised for 5 in the poise category? Won't you feel foolish when I ask you if you missed the fact that Martin never stopped cracking his knuckles? Students only make that mistake once.

- "Student scoring might damage self-esteem." The best way to build self-esteem is to try something difficult and succeed, not to be told that every effort is praiseworthy. If teachers set up their classes to understand that we are all emerging speakers, no student will feel bad because of an initial subpar performance. "Martin Luther King Jr. might have gotten all 5s," you can remind them, "but I don't expect that kind of mastery. We know going in that it is tough to put life into a speech, so don't panic if you get a 2 rating." Their self-esteem will soar when they see the hands go up at 4 in the next speech.

- "Grades should never be public." Please note that we don't make the speaker's *grade* public. A speech with ratings of 3s and 4s may well be an A speech, once the teacher's marks are factored in. For the most part, I agree that grades should not be publicized. But this is a unique situation. This is *public* speaking. Remember the goal: to prepare students to be confident and comfortable oral communicators in the interview, office, boardroom, and so on. Students need to know how an audience sees them. They need to become comfortable with the idea that in the real world, the listeners' opinions matter.

CREATING EFFECTIVE RUBRICS

After the initial immediate feedback, the student should receive another evaluation—the scores on the rubric or score sheet handed out when the project was assigned. In Chapter 2, I examined a generic speaking rubric created by a district's language arts department. Most teachers, however, create their own rubrics and score sheets for the speaking activities in their classes. Over the years, I have collected quite a few of these. I want to spend some time analyzing two examples that I think are fairly representative. Figure 15.1 shows a rubric created by a fourth-grade teacher.

FIGURE 15.1: ORAL BOOK REPORT ON HISTORICAL FICTION

Book Report components complete and on time (10 points)	
There is an interesting opening and a satisfying conclusion (10 points)	
Speak loudly, clearly, and slowly (10 points)	
Make eye contact with the audience (10 points)	
The character in the story is creatively shown to the audience with historical facts, motivation, and expression (20 points)	
Preparation and practice are evident (10 points)	
Presentation is organized and within the time limit (3–4 minutes) (minimum = 3 min./maximum = 4 min.) (15 points)	
Keep audience engaged and interested (5 points)	
Costume and/or props (10 points)	
Total Points (100 possible)	

Exemplary	A	90–100
Competent	B	80–89
Developing	C	70–79
Emerging	D	60–69

Below 69: Has little understanding of writing or speaking process

Having read this far, you can see some issues with Figure 15.1. Let's examine it piece by piece to see what problems we can discover and avoid in the future.

Notice that the first box has nothing to do with oral presentation. It is a score for timeliness and work ethic. The students had to turn in answers to questions as they read the book, which was a way for the teacher to see if they were on track.

The second box addresses an aspect of building a speech: organization. Two pieces of that are included, the opening and the closing. I am not sure the descriptors are useful for children. "Interesting?" "Satisfying?" To whom? These adjectives invite a discussion of audience analysis.

The third box shifts to aspects of performing a speech. Actually, three very different aspects of performance—volume, enunciation, and speed—are grouped into one 10-point category. We wouldn't score a piece of writing using a rubric that put "organization, word choice, and spelling" in one category, and, in scoring speeches, we need to be equally clear to separate the distinct skills.

The fourth box contains another element from the performance category that commonly shows up in rubrics. Every teacher realizes that eye contact is part of effective communication. I have no complaint about including it, but I wonder if the teacher included specific lessons about eye contact.

The fifth box is problematic. Worth double the points of eye contact, a book's character must be "creatively shown," another sloppy descriptor. What would that mean in the eyes of a student? And how do I creatively show "with historical facts, motivation, and expression"? I suspect the rubric creator is trying to get at the content part of building a speech. Perhaps the project requirements include using a certain number of historical facts in the presentation and explaining the main character's motivation. That should be made clear and scored separately as "content." "Expression" (what we now refer to as "life") is actually an element of performing a speech and should not be grouped with content/building a speech.

What would be evidence of "preparation and practice" in box six? I have seen speakers who worked hard, yet nerves got the better of them and their performance suffered. I have seen natural showmen perform well extemporaneously. What, specifically, do I look for when assessing preparation and practice?

In box seven, we again run into the problem of grouping unrelated elements. Organization (building a speech) should be scored separately from timing. A student may have brilliant signposts and a clear beginning, middle, and end, but he may take four and a half minutes to say all of that. What then? How many points do I give the child with excellent organization but who exceeds four minutes? I also note that the other parts of organization, the opening and closing, were isolated and put into box two.

Only five points are awarded for what is perhaps the real test of all oral communication: keeping the audience engaged and interested. Beyond that problem, I wonder how the teacher prepared students for knowing how to engage a particular audience.

Finally, we are back to an aspect of building a speech (appearance) when students get points for their costumes.

Just taking the elements this teacher values and using her words, we could greatly improve the rubric simply by reorganizing it. Using the framework we now have, the rubric could be restructured as shown in Figure 15.2.

FIGURE 15.2: REVISED RUBRIC FOR ORAL BOOK REPORT ON HISTORICAL FICTION

BUILDING A SPEECH

Audience (5 points) "Interested and engaged"	
Content (25 points) "Historical facts" Character "motivation" "3–4 minutes" of content	
Organization (20 points) "Interesting opening" "Organized" body of speech "Satisfying ending"	
Visual Aids (5 points) "Props" meaningful and well made	
Appearance (5 points) "Costume" accurate for time period	

PERFORMING A SPEECH

Voice (10 points) Speaks "loudly" Speaks "clearly"	
Life (10 points) "Expression"	
Eye Contact (5 points)	
Speed (5 points) Speaks "slowly"	

In Figure 15.2, some key elements are missing, but reworking the rubric puts us on track to giving more understandable feedback. A student could easily see areas of strength and weakness. One student might notice that she is strong at writing a speech but weak at delivering one. Another student might notice that he is generally good at giving a speech but speaks too fast. Yet another student might realize that she is good at organizing but less adept at including all the necessary content. This would be a great improvement upon the original rubric.

Figure 15.3 is a rubric created by a ninth-grade science teacher who required students to present articles about "science-related occurrences" in the news.

FIGURE 15.3: RUBRIC FOR SCIENCE PRESENTATION

1. Oral Presentation

make eye contact with the class	5 pts.	_____
speak loud enough for class to hear	5 pts.	_____
hold head up	5 pts.	_____
use note cards	5 pts.	_____
knowledgeable	5 pts.	_____

2. Written Presentation

5 W's answered	20 pts.	_____

3. Display

written work is mounted on poster	5 pts.	_____
articles are cut out neatly	5 pts.	_____
display is colorful	5 pts.	_____
display includes hand-drawn map, picture, flag, etc. (use your imagination)	15 pts.	_____

Again, I am sure you can see where there is room for improvement in Figure 15.3. This is the only rubric I have ever seen that gives a score for holding the head up, but if it gets us to the idea that poise is important, I am all for it. One element of voice is present ("speak loud enough"), so we have a beginning there, also. The idea that a speech needs to contain some life is totally missing, but the rubric understands the need to include eye contact. I am not sure about "use note cards." Perhaps it means "use note cards *well*," which may make it another way of reinforcing the need for eye contact. Gestures and speed have been ignored.

I suggest that "knowledgeable" is getting at the content part of building a speech. Parts 2 and 3 are also about content. Certainly we could argue about the relative point values here (is a hand drawing worth three times as much as being knowledgeable?), but I will leave that aside.

A little reorganization could improve the initial rubric (see Figure

15.4).

FIGURE 15.4: REVISED RUBRIC FOR SCIENCE PRESENTATION

BUILDING A SPEECH

Content (25 points) "knowledgeable…" "5 W's"	
Visual Aids (25 points) "on poster" "cut neatly" "colorful" "hand-drawn"	

PERFORMING A SPEECH

Poise (5 points) "hold head up"	
Voice (5 points) "speak loud enough"	
Eye Contact (10 points) "make eye contact" "use note cards well"	

When the rubric is reorganized, it is easy to see what was left out. If a student did all that was asked of him in this rubric, he would still fall far short of what is needed to meet the speaking standards. But that may be fine. Not all speeches have to include all elements of effective oral communication. Perhaps you want to have students deliver a speech and focus only on life and eye contact. Maybe you want students to work hard on using signposts, building content, and performing in a poised manner. I have no problem with those ideas. Just don't randomly jumble disparate speaking skills.

I encourage you to examine the speaking rubrics and score sheets you currently use in the same way we scrutinized the examples in Figures 15.1, 15.2, 15.3, and 15.4. I am sure yours have good points, just as these samples did, and that some small adjustments will make the evaluations more useful for students.

PUSHING FOR MORE PRECISION

The skills of oral expression should not be defined differently in Mrs. Smith's and Mr. Johnson's fourth-grade classes, in Mr. Janicki's social studies class and Mr. Avery's English class, in Ms. Mooney's sixth-grade class and Ms. Pond's eleventh-grade class. It's often the case that last year's teacher said a good speech should include a costume, eye contact, speaking loudly, and historical facts; this year's teacher said a good speech includes content, eye contact, expression, a good opening, and visual aids; and next year's teacher will say a good speech includes understanding the topic, standing up straight, eye contact, loud volume, not saying "um" and "uh," and speaking distinctly. Over the years our students get an idea of what it takes to be an effective oral communicator, but if we were more consistent, they would master the skills. It will be easier for them to meet the oral expression standards if all of their teachers use the same language. Let me suggest some new generic rubrics and score sheets that can be easily modified as the grade levels and subjects warrant and that will provide a consistent framework for students as they move through the educational system and beyond.

We can start by creating evaluations that reflect the two main parts of all oral communication. The basic structure could look like Figure 15.5. Teachers who like to assign points could make the categories worth whatever value they wish.

FIGURE 15.5: BASIC RUBRIC FOR PUBLIC SPEAKING

BUILDING A SPEECH	
Audience	
Content	
Organization	
Visual aids	
Appearance	

PERFORMING A SPEECH	
Poise	
Voice	
Life	
Eye contact	
Gestures	
Speed	

Within the basic structure of Figure 15.5, teachers can add descriptors of the important requirements. In the next class or next grade level, while the descriptors may change, the basic understanding of the components of a good speech remains the same. Figure 15.6 shows two examples of how the content box can be adapted, depending on the assignment.

FIGURE 15.6: MODIFYING THE CONTENT SECTION

Content
   Name of invention
   Name of inventor(s)
   Date of invention
   Needs met by invention
   Benefit to our lives	

Content
   Name of case
   Date of decision
   Facts of case
   Reason for decision
   How decision affects us today	

For teachers who assign multiple speeches within the year, the same score sheets can be used and easily modified. The majority of the components of effective oral communication don't change from speech to speech. For instance, the requirements of organization don't change from speech to speech, nor do the expectations of eye contact. This means that the basic rubric form, once built, is applicable in a wide range of activities (see Figure 15.7).

FIGURE 15.7: ENHANCED RUBRIC FOR ORAL COMMUNICATION

BUILDING A SPEECH	
Audience Speech appropriate for audience (5 points) Key points clarified (5) Connectors present (5)	
Content (varies from speech to speech)	
Organization Grabber opening immediately engaged listeners (5 points) Well-chosen organizational structure (5) Signposts clearly stated (5) Powerful closing (5)	
Visual aids (varies)	
Appearance (varies)	
PERFORMING A SPEECH	
Poise Speaker appeared calm and confident (5) No distracting behaviors (5)	
Voice Loud enough for the space (5) Every word clear (5) No odd vocal mannerisms (5)	
Life Could hear feeling in voice (5) Avoided sounding monotonous (5)	

Eye contact Looked at each member of audience at some point (5) Did not focus only on teacher or a few students (5)	
Gestures Used hands in meaningful ways (5) Facial expressions contributed to speech (5) Body gestures helped message (5)	
Speed Not too fast (5) Adjusted speed to enhance message (5) Pauses created dramatic effect (5)	

Naturally, the language within the boxes of Figure 15.7 can be modified as appropriate for your students; number values can be adjusted to emphasize the parts you think are most important. Using a score sheet like this will give students a clear picture of their strengths and weaknesses, just as the multiple-trait rubric for writing increases students' understanding of strengths and weaknesses in their written work.

The same elements can be structured differently to fit the requirements in most districts. While there is no agreement nationwide on the labels (e.g., advanced, proficient, basic, pre-basic; advanced, proficient, partially proficient, in-progress), a four-point rubric can and should be developed using the framework I've described. The rubric for performing a speech, once created for each grade level, will work across the curriculum. Figure 15.8 shows an example of a rubric from a workshop I conducted with ninth-grade teachers. Notice that the content box is generic, allowing the rubric to be used in a variety of assignments. Figure 15.9 shows the performance rubric they created to use in all classes.

FIGURE 15.8: MULTIPURPOSE SPEAKING RUBRIC

Notice that some wording is the same in multiple boxes. For example, to be an advanced speaker organizationally, a student needs an opening that grabs the listener and a powerful closing; the proficient speaker must also have both of those. These teachers felt that what distinguished advanced from proficient in organization was the use of signposts, so that is the only language that differed from one box to the next. I agreed with them. It is not the case that all language needs to change from one level to the next. Often, to achieve the next level requires mastering the same skills *plus* one thing more. In this case, proficient *and* advanced speakers must master openings and closings, but the advanced must also master signposts.

FIGURE 15.8: MULTIPURPOSE SPEAKING RUBRIC (CONTINUED)

BUILDING A SPEECH	4 ADVANCED	3 PROFICIENT
AUDIENCE	• speech perfectly designed for this specific audience • key points understandable • several clear connections to this audience	• speech clearly designed for this audience • one or two points or key terms should have been more clearly explained • two or three attempts to connect with the audience
CONTENT	• all required content included • purpose of speech clear • no extraneous material included	• all required content included • purpose of speech clear • some extraneous material
ORGANIZATION	• good choice of organizational structure • opening grabbed the listeners • explicit and frequent signposts • powerful closing	• good choice of organizational structure • opening grabbed the listeners • some signposts • powerful closing
VISUAL AIDS	• visual aids relevant • aids clarified important concepts • aids appropriate for the audience and the room • well designed	• visual aids relevant • aids clarified important concepts • aids understandable for most of the audience • most of the audience could see the aids • well designed
APPEARANCE	• student looked sharp • dress appropriate for the speech • added something above and beyond expectations	• student looked sharp • dress appropriate for the speech

2 BASIC	1 EMERGING
• little evidence that speech designed for this audience • several key points needed explanation • only one attempt to connect	• no evidence that particular audience considered • no attempt to explain things for this audience • no connectors
• most required content included • audience could figure out the purpose • unnecessary information presented • verbal viruses present but not problematic	• important omissions of required content • unable to understand purpose of speech • random information in speech • verbal viruses detracted from speech
• good choice of organizational structure • ineffective opening • infrequent signposts • ineffective closing	• disorganized • ineffective opening • no signposts • speech just stopped
• visual aids relevant • aids merely repeated what was said • aids appropriate for most of the audience • many audience members could not see the aids • decorations and/or sloppiness diminished aids' appearance	• no visual aid or irrelevant aids • sloppy and hard to see
• student took care to adjust appearance before speech	• no attempt to change appearance for the occasion

FIGURE 15.9: PERFORMANCE RUBRIC

PVLEGS	4 ADVANCED	3 PROFICIENT
POISE	• student calm and confident • no distracting behaviors • no shuffling, fidgeting, wiggling	• student calm and confident • only one or two distracting behaviors that did not diminish overall performance
VOICE	• voice perfect for the room • every word clear and distinct	• voice perfect for the room • a few words blurred/indistinct
LIFE	• great expression • many emotions expressed • excellent feeling	• good expression • some feeling evident in parts of speech
EYE CONTACT	• looked at each member of the audience at some point • eye contact continuous	• looked at each member of the audience • eye contact made for most of the speech
GESTURES	• excellent use of hands for descriptive and emphatic purposes • facial expressions added to message • body language contributed to message	• good use of hands • some facial gestures • limited body language
SPEED	• not too fast or too slow • varied pacing to enhance message • paused for dramatic effect	• not too fast or too slow • some attempt to adjust pace for effect • no pauses

2 BASIC	1 EMERGING
• student somewhat ill-at-ease • occasionally distracted the audience	• student ill-at-ease • many and repeated distracting behaviors greatly detracting from performance
• voice a bit too soft/loud • several words and phrases indistinct	• had a hard time hearing the speech • many words and phrases unclear
• some attempt at expression • some attempt at adding emotion in speech	• tone monotonous • no expression • no attempt to add feeling to voice
• looked at most members of the audience • looked at notes too much	• script-bound • never looked at most of audience
• some hand gestures • facial expressions and body language minimal	• no gestures • no attempt to use facial expression • no use of body motions
• not too fast or too slow • no attempt to adjust pace • no pauses	• spoke too quickly • no pacing or pauses

The descriptors in the rubric boxes will change depending on the grade level. What is advanced poise for a first grader (few wiggles, minimal fidgeting) is quite different than advanced poise for an eleventh grader (no wiggles, no fidgeting). You (and your colleagues) can craft language appropriate for your students. Look for more sample rubrics at www.pvlegs.com. If you have a rubric to share, please send it to me to post.

CHAPTER 16:

Speaking Activities Across the Curriculum

I t doesn't matter what subject is being taught—math, science, social studies, language arts, health, industrial technology, Spanish, art—all classes involve speaking. The activity ideas in this chapter can be adapted to any subject area. I have avoided mentioning activities that I think we all know about: book reports, research projects, biography projects, and so on. Those are so common that I don't need to tell you how they work. Instead, I offer some varied ways that I have taught public speaking in classes. Some may be new to you or add a different twist to a familiar activity. In the parentheses following each subheading, I have indicated the speaking skill(s) most relevant to the activity. I hope you'll try some of these activities in your class as you expand your teaching of public speaking.

1. MODELING MARTIN LUTHER KING, JR. (ALL)

I was a young boy when I first heard Martin Luther King Jr. speak, and he quickly became my hero. Every year that I taught, I used his "I Have a Dream" speech to show students the power of public speaking. The text can be found easily online and in several books in your library. Read it with your students.

Ask students to think about the *audience* King had to address and the complexity of his challenge: blacks who supported him in his peace movement, and blacks who were becoming militant and violent; whites who supported him, and whites who were screaming at him; lawmakers he wanted to move to action. Ask students to look for places in the speech that address each of those audience segments. Notice the connectors. Where does King indicate that he understands the audience's perspective?

Examine the *content*. What was his purpose in speaking? What are his main points?

Review the *organization* of the speech. It's a brilliant composition. Everyone knows the repetition of the phrase, "I have a dream," but few realize that King used a similar organizational strategy throughout the speech. "One hundred years later," "we can never be satisfied," and "let freedom ring" are also repeated, breaking the speech into memorable sections.

Although King used no overt *visual aids,* his appearance was important. If possible, show students a video of King delivering his "I Have a Dream" speech from the Lincoln Memorial. How did he dress? Why did he always wear a black suit, white shirt, and black tie?

You can also discuss the *performance*. Talk about the *poise* King demonstrated in front of 500,000 people and a television audience. Discuss the power of his voice. *Life*? He is one of the most dynamic speakers your students will ever hear. Eye contact and gestures aren't a major part of this speech because of the venue. Point that out. Also discuss King's tremendous use of *speed and pacing* for effect. Analyzing this speech is a unique way to celebrate Martin Luther King Day and any other occasion of the year.

2. ANALYZE OTHER SPEAKERS (ALL)

Your students will analyze other speakers for you. They will come into your class and say, "Did you see the president's speech last night?" or "Did you see Miss South Carolina?" Once students become aware of the art of public speaking, they will analyze all of the performances they see. Look at newscasters, TV hosts, and other speakers, and spend a few minutes discussing their PVLEGS.

3. THINK, PAIR, SHARE (CONTENT, EYE CONTACT)

Provide a thought-provoking question to the class. The question could be related to a unit of study, but it also might be a random but engaging question. Give students a few moments to think about the question, and then ask them to find a partner. I always like to have the kids decide which one of them will be Person A and which Person B. Once that is decided, I say, "Okay, B, you go first. Explain to your partner your thinking in response to our question." After a couple of minutes, I say, "Okay, B, you stop and let A explain." The idea is to get them to come to a consensus about the answer to the question. Have them think about the statements that seemed the most valuable in reaching agreement. Finally, the entire class regroups for a discussion.

For the whole-class discussion, some days I say, "Person A will talk today. If you are Person A, tell us what you and your partner decided." Some days I call on Person B. This eliminates the problem of having only the highly verbal students dominate the discussion.

4. WHAT HAPPENED HERE? (LIFE)

Find interesting photographs from newspapers and magazines. Build a large collection of these odd photos. Ask students to think of a brief story that would explain the photo. How did the shoe end up on top of that pole? How did the child get his head stuck in that chair? Call on volunteers to share their ideas focusing on the speaking skill of life.

5. BROWN BAG INTRODUCTIONS (VISUAL AIDS)

This is a great idea for a get-to-know-you activity at the beginning of the year. Tell students to bring in a brown lunch bag that contains five or six items that represent who they are. The items could be pictures, equipment they use, mini versions of objects that are important to them, and so on. Each student takes a turn at the front of the class and reveals the contents while explaining the significance of the items. Remind students of the effective ways to use visual aids while speaking.

6. SHOW AND TELL (VISUAL AIDS)

This is really retro . . . but really engaging. When I taught eighth grade, I was surprised when a student came to me and asked if she could bring in something to show her classmates. I said yes, and after her presentation, many other students asked if *they* could bring in something. I thought about it. Show and tell might cost me five minutes, but the benefits are huge. It lets kids be kids; it creates connections between kids; it improves class atmosphere; it lets students showcase their lives outside of school; it helps the teacher connect with the students. It is also another chance to work on presentation skills, in particular, the use of visual aids while speaking. Give each speaker advice on how to present the item in a way that all students can appreciate it, for example.

7. DIGITAL STORYTELLING (LIFE, CONTENT, ORGANIZATION)

Many more opportunities for oral expression exist because of free online tools and inexpensive cameras and recorders. While it is always dangerous to list Web sites—by the time you get to print, the site is gone, has added a fee, or been outdone by a newer site—I will mention a couple that offer interesting and engaging options. Personal stories, book talks, creative writing assignments, third-person retelling, and more can all be done with images and voice recording. At Animoto (www.animoto.com), pictures and video clips can be uploaded and sound can be added. At ZooBurst (www.zooburst.com), students can create online "pop-up" books and record their voices to animate the character in the book they create. Sites such as PhotoPeach (www.photopeach.com) and Imageloop (www.imageloop.com) allow students to upload photos and make slideshows with sound. With digital recorders such as Flip and Bloggie cameras that have built-in USB arms, students can make videos and instantly upload them to a class wiki or Web page. In addition to offering a speaking opportunity beyond getting up in front of the class, the excitement of speaking in front of a potentially large audience—anyone with access to the site—and the excitement of having immortality—the in-class speech lasts three minutes but the posted video lasts forever—can motivate many students to become more verbal. The traditional "What I Did This Summer" essay becomes an online slideshow or video with student narration. Follow your school's or district's policies about online safety.

8. ONLINE DISCUSSIONS (CONTENT, LIFE, AUDIENCE)

Certainly class discussions will improve with improved speaking skills. Those discussions can move beyond the classroom and into the online world with free tools in the "cloud." VoiceThread (www.voicethread.com) allows users to upload images and video and record comments about them. Then visitors to the created page can record responses and continue the discussion. For example, a teacher could upload an image of an oil-covered bird and start a discussion of offshore drilling. Students could be given an assignment to access the page, respond to the image, and react specifically to the comments of at least two classmates. Students who are quiet in class often blossom when given a chance to speak in this arena. Unlike a class discussion, the comment can be practiced, and the comment can be deleted if a mistake is made. Students will quickly realize that a good point becomes a great point if it's passionately spoken.

9. PODCASTING (LIFE)

Many students have computers with the ability to make podcasts. Most Apple computers come with a software program called GarageBand, which makes it extremely easy to produce a broadcast with voice and pictures that can be sent via e-mail or downloaded to an MP3 player or iPod. You don't have to teach GarageBand—many of your students are already masters. Just let them turn in a podcast sometimes instead of another chapter summary paragraph.

Web sites such as Gabcast (www.gabcast.com) enable students to use their cell phones to make podcasts. If you register with the site, students can write a speech, dial an 800 number, record the speech, and then send the speech to a computer. If they send it to your classroom computer, you can play it for the class or post it on a class Web page or blog. It is an enormously engaging assignment: "I get to use my cell phone in class?!" At Vocaroo's Web site (www.vocaroo.com), students can make a voice recording with any computer that has a built-in or attached microphone. These recordings can also be e-mailed or embedded in a Web page or a wiki. Using these online recording sites offers great lessons in inflection. Students are stunned to see how a disembodied voice sounds, and they quickly erase their first recording and try again until the life comes through.

10. TRAVELING DEBATES (VOICE, AUDIENCE, CONTENT, EYE CONTACT, POISE)

Traveling debates can be used in any subject. The teacher poses a question. Should the character in the novel have done that? Should the United States have invaded Iraq? Should we allow cloning? Should cigarettes be banned? Come up with some content-related questions that have two strong sides. Then tell the class to stand up and move: "Stand on this side of the room if you think that we should have physical education every day. Stand on that side of the room if you think we should not have P.E. every day."

It is not important to have an even number of students on each side. In fact, sometimes it is more fun to have five students against twenty-five students. As long as there are people on each side, you can begin. (No, no one can be in the middle—we either have P.E. every day or we don't. Make students decide.)

The rules are simple. One person speaks at a time. I address the side with the smaller number and let someone from that side speak first for up to two minutes. The speaker tries to persuade students from the other side to walk over to his side. There is no clapping, no voting, and no commenting—if your viewpoint has changed, you simply move over to the other side of the room. When students finish moving (*if* they move—sometimes no one is persuaded), call on a student from the opposing side of the room. Her goal is the same: to get students to switch sides. Call on different students from each side several times. Here's how the P.E. debate might go:

> PRO: We should have P.E. every day because Americans are getting fat. Schools teach you stuff to make your life better like reading and stuff, so they should make you exercise 'cuz that is good for you.

> (*No one moves.*)

> CON: We should not have P.E. Lots of us play sports outside of school, and we get exercise on our own. P.E. is dumb anyhow. We just play dumb games no one likes.

(*Two kids switch over to the con side of the room.*)

PRO: What would you rather do, go to math class or go play a game in P.E.? P.E. gets us out of other classes. Sometimes, we even get to go outside.

(*Ten kids switch sides, including one of the two who just came over.*)

Traveling debates emphasize audience, because to be successful at moving students by coming up with a winning argument, you have to understand your listeners. To point out that exercise reduces cholesterol may not be persuasive to fifth graders. Eye contact is essential; looking right at someone is powerful if you are trying to move him or her. Of course, students will primarily look at the teacher, as always. Stress that you are not going to move anywhere. Students need to talk to the peers they want to persuade.

11. FREEZE FRAME (LIFE, GESTURES, VOICE)

Improvisation games can be a lot of fun in class. Many involve quick thinking and quick wit, but Freeze Frame is useful for practicing some of our speaking skills. Choose two student volunteers. Assign them parts to play in a two-person drama. For example, ask one student to be the parent and the other the child who has just taken the parent's toothbrush to brush the dog's teeth. This forces students to play with life in their voices. In this case, the students have to speak like an angry mom or a young child.

When you say, "Action!" the play begins. Let the volunteers act out the scene for a couple of minutes. At some point, say, "Freeze!" The two actors must stop in the exact position they were in when they heard "freeze" and hold that position. Try to stop them when they are in an interesting position. Perhaps the mom is holding up the imaginary toothbrush to show the child how damaged it is, and the child has his arms crossed.

Now for the tricky part. Choose a volunteer to replace one of the two frozen characters. The new volunteer can take the place of whichever character she wants, but she must assume the exact position of the actor being replaced. The new actor will speak first when you say, "Action!"

but she must change the scene. It is no longer a mom, a child, and a toothbrush scene. The new actor has to use the gesture she inherited and go off in a new direction. The actor who wasn't replaced has to go along with whatever idea the new actor thought of. The following scene picks up from just after the new actor joins the scene:

TEACHER: Action!

NEW PLAYER: (*Holding hand up exactly as the "mom" did.*) As you can see, I have here a magic wand. This wand will make the straightjacket mysteriously fall away! Kazaam!

OLD PLAYER: (*Hands were crossed but now swing open.*) Wow! That is amazing! How did you do it?

NEW PLAYER: A magician never tells. Now help me with this new trick. Pick a card, any card. (*Holding hands out as if to display a spread-out deck of cards.*)

OLD PLAYER: (*Reaching for a card.*) Okay, I'll choose . . .

TEACHER: Freeze! Who wants to volunteer to replace one of these two?

(*A second new player comes in and takes the place of the old player reaching out.*)

TEACHER: Action!

SECOND NEW PLAYER: Here is the money. You say these treasure maps are all good?

FIRST NEW PLAYER: (*Speaking like a pirate.*) Arrr, yes. Each one came from my days on the pirate ship.

I have used this game very successfully with students from grades six through twelve. There is a bit of a learning curve. You must make sure the scene goes in a new direction when the new student comes in, and you must make sure the new character uses the inherited gesture. The new player can't come in and just ignore the position he assumed. If his hand is outstretched when he takes the position of the previous actor, he has to do something with an outstretched hand. Sometimes you may stop a scene, and no one will volunteer because no one has an idea of what to do. Very soon, though, students will begin to see that dynamic, dramatic gestures are the most fun to work with, and they will begin to free up their motions. You will become a better director, too, and will begin to see which positions offer the best potential and, hence, the best time to yell, "Freeze!"

Sure, some students are better than others. Some students have a slew of character voices they are dying to use; some love to get up and do crazy things; conversely, some are too shy to play but love to watch and laugh. In all cases, my students have loved the game. They would ask to play any time we had a few extra minutes. It kept me sane on indoor recess days.

12. OBJECT BOX (VISUAL AIDS)

Put some small, silly items in a box: a piece of yarn, a marshmallow, a key, a feather, a sponge—crazy things. Choose a student to reach into the box and, without looking, pull something out. Give the student two minutes to prepare a speech that somehow incorporates the item. Here are some examples.

> *Ah, my favorite sweater. This is all that is left now, just this one piece of yarn. But when I was younger, it was part of my favorite piece of clothing.*

> *Here at the yarn factory we make all kinds of yarn. Our most popular yarn is this one right here. We call this color Ocean Mist.*

13. TWO TRUTHS AND A LIE (LIFE, CONTENT)

At the beginning of the year ask students to pair up. Give students a few minutes to interview each other. Each pair will then come up to the front of the room to introduce each other. The trick is that the introducing student must include three statements about her partner, one of which is not true. The objective is to fool the listeners, who will be asked to determine which statement is the lie. The speaker must be poised, or else her listeners will easily discover the lie. (The student being introduced has to be poised as well in order to remain impassive when he hears the lie.) The exercise encourages students to think carefully about content: what are the two most interesting things to tell the class, and what lie would fit in? It won't fool many people if you say, "Bill has two sisters named Karen and Ally. He has a dog named Bowser. He has twelve arms." Students need to consider content that would be believable and deliver it in the same style as the factual content.

14. DEMONSTRATION SPEECH . . . WITHOUT ANY PROPS (GESTURES, EYE CONTACT)

Tell students they will have to demonstrate how to do something. For example, they can demonstrate how to make a paper airplane, how to brush teeth, how to make a peanut butter sandwich, how to bake brownies, or how to fix a flat tire. The trick is that when they do the presentation, they can't use any visual aids. They have to gesture so well that we "see" the props without them being there:

> *Notice that I have a plain piece of white paper, 8 1/2 by 11 inches. (Holding right hand out with two fingers pinched together and using left hand to point to the invisible paper hanging down from the pinched fingers.) First, fold the paper in half. (Left hand goes 11 inches below the pinched fingers of the right hand, pinches the bottom of the invisible paper, and brings the pinched edge up to the right hand.)*

Students enjoy using their imaginations to fill in the blanks. They also enjoy keeping track of the "props" and noticing any slipups on the part of a speaker. During a student's demonstration about how to make brownies, for example, the audience will notice if she "pours" the batter into the pan as if the pan were on the right edge of the desk but then "picks it up" to put in the "oven" as if it were on the left edge of the desk. Through this activity, students will realize how important even subtle gestures can be.

15. POETRY CAFÉ (LIFE, POISE, VOICE, SPEED)

At the end of her poetry unit, my teaching teammate always held a poetry café. Students found a favorite poem (or, in some cases, wrote a poem), which they read aloud. To make it more significant, parents were invited, students volunteered to bring food and drinks, the room was rearranged, and everyone was required to dress up. Students would take turns sitting on the stool in the center of the room to recite their poems. Adding the performance piece encourages students to become much more animated readers. It was great P.R. (parents and administrators loved it), and students who had little interest in poetry at the start of the unit became really enthusiastic about poetry and this culminating activity.

16. COMMERCIALS (ALL)

The school district I worked in decided to make a deal with the Coca-Cola Company. The district got millions of dollars to agree to offer Coke products and only Coke products in all of the schools. Coca-Cola supplied juices and water in all school cafeterias and soft drinks in all teachers' lounge vending machines. This gave me the idea of having *all* classes sponsored by some product. Why not have the Texas Instruments Pre-calculus Hour? The Frito Lay Language Arts Period? Civics—Brought to You by Hostess? Students were thrilled with the idea.

Students volunteered to do a thirty-second spot during a future class period. They had a week or so to prepare. As for a true commercial, thirty seconds was the exact time allowed—they could not go one second over, and if they finished early, they had to stand in front of the class until thirty seconds lapsed. I let students invent their own products or use existing products. Then, during class, I would have a commercial break presented by a student—perhaps as we were transitioning from one activity to another or at the end of the class.

TEACHER: Today's class has been brought to you by Kevin. Kevin?

KEVIN: Are you tired of homework? Meet the Droid 2020 Homework Application. This app will . . .

The commercials were a minimal intrusion into my class and a lot of fun for the speakers and the listeners.

17. READING ALOUD (LIFE, VOICE)

Many teachers have students read sections of a book aloud for a class. One student reads the first section of a textbook, another reads the second section, and so on. If you do this in your class, insist that students read with life in their voices and don't allow the droning that is so common. Just set this up as a class expectation—if you read, you will read with feeling. Yes, it is easier to read with feeling if you are reading a passage from a novel rather than a textbook, but monotones are never acceptable.

Many teachers also schedule reader's theater. In some versions, students take the parts of characters in a chosen book and deliver lines of dialogue. Find a section of a novel that has a long conversation between characters. Students become the characters as they read. Instead of Heassam and Jeremy from our class reading aloud, we are listening to story characters, and students have to add the life of the characters to their voices.

Afterword

Years ago the comedian Don Novello would take the stage as Guido Sarducci, an Italian monk. In one of his routines Guido talks about the "Five-Minute University" he created. The idea was simple: Classes are only five minutes long because in five minutes you can learn what the average college graduate remembers five years after leaving campus. "Economics class? Supply and demand."

It's a funny routine, and I encourage you to look it up on YouTube. But I also find the premise disturbing. I saw the routine for the first time when I was still teaching science and had just finished a unit on cells. I suddenly wondered how long the students would remember "Golgi bodies." I also had to wonder about the lasting value of other subjects I taught. As teachers, we don't know the long-term impact of our efforts, but I have never doubted the importance of teaching speaking skills.

My last teaching assignment was at a middle school that shared a campus with a high school. Let me tell you about a conversation that I had with Martin and Michelle, two of my former students.

> **MARTIN:** Mr. Palmer! We had to give speeches in ninth-grade English.
>
> **MICHELLE:** Yeah, you could tell the kids who had you. Our speeches were so much better.
>
> **MARTIN:** I know. It was so much easier! I really did well. Do you still make students do the Supreme Court speech?
>
> **MICHELLE:** I was so scared at that! Now it seems really easy. Do you still do traveling debates?

MARTIN: I *loved* traveling debates. Do you remember the time . . .

We get caught up in the day-to-day challenges of teaching and seldom have time for reflection. I know that. But pause a minute right now and think about the future. What will be essential to your students' success? What skills will be called upon most often? Creativity? Reading? Collaboration? Perseverance? Writing? We could endlessly debate the most essential skills, but I am confident that most of us would include oral communication on that list.

Now think about *your* life. Would *you* have liked more instruction in public speaking when you were in school? Would *you* have benefited from the ideas contained in this book? I encourage you, then, to give your students a lifelong benefit by teaching speaking.

APPENDIX:
FREQUENTLY ASKED QUESTIONS

Over the years, teachers have posed many questions about how to teach public speaking, so let me answer some that come up frequently. If you have other questions or concerns, feel free to contact me through my Web site, www.pvlegs.com.

What about the student who is shy?

We discussed the fact that many people fear public speaking. For some students, that fear is more intense than it is for others. You probably have one or two students in each class who are painfully shy. They come up to you and say, "I don't think I can do this" in a tiny voice. You reply, "Oh, well. Your presentation is on November 5." Okay, maybe not quite as blunt as that. The reality is that you have students who hate math or poetry or writing. If they come up to you and say, "This is hard for me, and I hate it," do you excuse them from the assignment or the unit? No, you work them through the fear: "I believe in you. I know this is tough for you, but you can do it. This is really important. I want you to get over the fear now, so you can succeed when it really counts in life. It will be tough, but you can do this." In twenty years in the classroom, I recall one student who was especially terrified. Even so, she got up and went to the front of the room. The speech was a disaster, full of terrible distractions and strange noises—not just "um" and "uh" but odd exhaling sounds as well. She was a basket case. But she did it. I almost got tears in my eyes when the class scored her. They knew how hard this was for her, and they adjusted their scores. I did get tears in my eyes when she came up to me absolutely beaming and said, "I did it! I did it!" Always give students a chance to succeed.

What do you do differently for special needs kids?

You modify as appropriate. Shorten the time limit. Modify the content required. Modify the grading. I remember Jeremy. He had some severe issues, and one manifestation of those was a very slow speaking pace. He labored to get words out. The average speaker might say 125 words a minute. Jeremy might say twenty-five. I still wanted him to have the experience of public speaking. It turned out to be another time the class proved to me how good they were at evaluating speeches. Without telling the class to modify their scoring, they did. For "speed," Jeremy got what I guess I should call a "Jeremy five" from the students, because they understood Jeremy and knew he did his best and had worked hard to get the words out.

Students in my school are struggling just to survive. Is this relevant to them?
The Colorado Student Assessment Program (CSAP) test included a question about onomatopoeia. Is that relevant? As a teacher, I often had the thought that some students had more important things to think about than my particular lesson. When your mother is in the last stages of cancer, how important is that lesson on gerunds? But I always know that no matter what happens in a life, that life will be better in some way by mastering oral communication skills. I can't take away from any student the opportunity to communicate better. For some, it may be their best chance at improving their lives.

Do you let students go out of the room to get ready?
For big presentations the standard rule in my class was that students could leave the room during the speech that preceded theirs. Some wanted to rehearse mentally one more time. Some wanted to change clothes. Some wanted a drink of water. Some wanted to do some of the calming exercises. I recommend letting students spend the five minutes before showtime outside the classroom door, unless it is a student you absolutely cannot trust.

Shouldn't we focus on the state-mandated test since that is what determines our school score?
Of course we should focus on the test. That is the current reality. But most of what is involved in speaking activities contributes to your test preparation. Creating content, organizing content, prewriting, outlining, condensing a large text into notes, research—all of these are great preparation for tests and everything else. The key is presenting these skills in a fresh way. There are only so many times you can write a ten-minute,

timed essay or read a paragraph and write a summary. Students who are nonwriters end up writing if you give them a new goal. Students who are tired of writing for no purpose become inspired when the writing is for a real audience. My students did as well or better on the district assessments as students in classes where speaking skills were not emphasized. As an aside, though, I never had one student thank me for moving him or her from "proficient low" to "proficient" on the CSAP, but I have had many, many students come back to my room years later to thank me for improving their oral communication.

Doesn't mimicking a student hurt her self-esteem?
Recall that I get up right after the students when we are talking about poise, and I mimic their actions. If they tugged at the shirt, I tug at the shirt, and the class laughs. If they twirl hair, I twirl my (imaginary) hair, and we have fun with that. I have never once in more than twenty years had a problem. First, students of all ages like to play. Second, I prequalified my volunteers: "Don't volunteer if you can't laugh at yourself. We all do dumb things, and we will have fun with the dumb things you do." I have found that using actual student examples is very effective in teaching, and exaggerating those examples has been a powerful way to drive home the lesson.

How do you differentiate?
Let me point out that giving a speaking assignment *is* differentiation. You have students who hate speaking. You also have students who love speaking and hate writing. Differentiation is not just about accommodating kinesthetic and logical/sequential learners. Let's accommodate verbal learners, too. For them, the chance to showcase their strengths motivates them to write well for the first time. Beyond that, I suppose I don't differentiate. I don't say to one student, "You are artistic, so instead of giving a speech, turn in a portfolio of drawings." When the student applies for a job as a graphic designer at some point in the future, he will have to speak well at the interview.

How do students react when they get low grades from the class?
No one likes to do poorly. How do your students react when they finish last at the track meet and their friends are watching? How do they react when some kids go off to calculus and they are in math basics? How do they react when they are put on the B team instead of the A team at your

school? I hope they react like they care. Of course they are disappointed. But they are also aware. They know that DeVaughn's speech was better than Mark's, just as they know Mark was faster than DeVaughn in the race. They realize there is room for improvement. They can handle this. Very rarely, a student is sure the class was wrong and that she was cheated. She knows she was a five in eye contact! Similar reactions happen sometimes when teachers hand back essays. The student who "knows" the paper deserves more than a C? With those students, the teacher should have an individual chat.

Do students retain the skills?
I think that question comes up because when students leave the classroom, they fall back into old habits. If you watch students in the lunchroom half an hour after they've done their presentations, you hear the verbal viruses, and if you see them answering a question in math class, they are slouched in their seats and speaking the way they always did. This is partly because habits are hard to break and partly because the students understand the audience. They *should* be different in the lunchroom. When it counts, they use the information.

When I taught in a middle school located right next to a high school, I always had students come back to visit, and often they told stories about having to give a speech in Mrs. English's class or Mr. History's class and how easy it was for them. "Do you still do the big Supreme Court speech? That was so hard! But tell the students it will be really useful in Mr. A.P. History's class." A parent of a former student who attended one of my workshops reported to me that her daughter Paige told her, "My teacher would never have made it in Mr. Palmer's class. His voice has no life, and he is so unpoised." Could my students recite all eleven elements of public speaking several years later? Probably not, though many will recall the PVLEGS poster I put up in the classroom (poise, voice, life, eye contact, gestures, speed). As a certainty, they remember the experience.

Isn't this too much to think about? How can a student remember all of these things?
If by "all of these things" the question refers to the six parts of performing a speech, I agree it is difficult. (The students don't have to remember the parts of building a speech—they have the information in front of them as they build the speech.) While performing, though, the student has to think

about poise *and* voice *and* life *and* eye contact *and* gestures *and* speed all at the same time. Most often, they are quite successful with one or two of those skills and the rest are weak. You can tell as they deliver the speeches that one student worked very hard on poise and eye contact and another worked hard on poise and gestures. Well done! They've each mastered two so far. The next speech, they can add one or two more. No one becomes a master speaker easily.

Remember also that sometimes you focus on only one skill: "In today's discussion, I want you to think about being poised. Next week, we will concentrate on life in your voices."

My school is making a big push toward twenty-first century skills. Speaking seems like an old skill, doesn't it?
First, remember what I said in Chapter 1, that Silicon Valley employers want better oral communication skills. It does not get more twenty-first century than Silicon Valley. Second, visit a Web site such as the one sponsored by the Partnership for 21st Century Skills (www.21stcenturyskills. org). Yes, information literacy, critical thinking, and problem solving are on the list of valued skills in this millennium. But communication is also on the list. This is an age in which corporations put their annual reports on podcasts instead of paper, and two business associates might have a video conference with the affiliates in Dubai and Singapore. Your speaking skills are on display more now than they have ever been. Finally, as schools incorporate twenty-first century tools as part of that push, speaking activities multiply. Digital storytelling, podcasts, and e-portfolios all demand effective oral communication.

I am not a master speaker. I'm not comfortable in front of crowds myself. How can I demonstrate all the skills mentioned?
Very few people are masterful speakers, just as very few people are great novelists. When I taught a lesson about metaphors, I was sure someone else could have come up with better metaphors than the ones I came up with. I don't have the writing talent of David Sedaris, but I think students still understood how and why we use metaphors. I didn't feel that I had to be a master writer to teach writing, and similarly, I don't think that I have to be a fantastic public speaker to give students instruction on speaking. You may not have the drama in your voice when you are demonstrating life that I have after decades of practice, but students will still enjoy the

lesson and understand the concept. Acknowledging that you, too, are scared in front of groups is a good way of connecting with students and making their feelings of anxiety okay.

Speaking skills are not part of my subject matter. Why should a (science, math, health . . .) teacher be involved?
Do students ever talk in your classroom? Do you ever have students present information in front of the class? Will your students ever leave school and compete in the global marketplace? Then speaking skills are part of your teaching responsibility.

I feel that when students are presenting there is less class control. Don't you think I should avoid situations like that in my classroom?
I assume that you *are* better at maintaining control of the class. But when the student is in front of the interview committee, you won't be there to control that situation for him. The class will not fall apart when students present. Often, students enjoy the break from seeing us all the time, and they definitely enjoy seeing peers perform. Some presentations will be weak, and attention will wander. That is a small price to pay for imparting speaking skills to your students.

I don't think parents care about speaking skills. Parents always ask about math and reading levels, but no one asks about speaking levels, do they?
Parents are aware of the standardized tests in the same way that teachers are. They know the newspaper will report scores for reading, writing, and math. When the National Assessment of Educational Progress (NAEP) test results come out, American students are compared to students in other countries in the areas of math and reading. Sometimes we see a report that compares our students to other countries' students in geography and science. I agree that *in schools* and *in the world of testing*, speaking skills have been off the radar (but that is changing!) and parents don't ask about them. Once you start teaching speaking, though, you will get many comments from parents who are thrilled with the inclusion of such an important life skill. Parents who come in to see presentations are excited to see their children speaking well. At conferences you will get many kudos for emphasizing communication skills, because while parents are aware of standardized tests, they are also very aware of life skills.

Do you let students practice during class time?

Occasionally. Sometimes students present as a team. I had students do newscasts; I had students work together in groups proposing new amendments to the Constitution. In situations such as these, it is natural for the team to want to see in advance the performance of a teammate. The team can provide excellent feedback to prepare an individual for her presentation. For individual speeches, I often paired students together and sent them out to practice. The hallway was filled with pairs of students—one earnestly but quietly orating, the other critiquing.

I am afraid to make students feel uncomfortable. Don't students feel uncomfortable speaking in front of the class?
For some reason, we care about comfort when we discuss public speaking. No student is comfortable sitting still for three hours and coloring circles on a standardized test. Many students are uncomfortable doing a timed writing, and others hate trying to draw a self-portrait in art class. It is definitely not comfortable to be stuck inside at a desk on a beautiful fall day. We have students do those things anyway. No one grows by doing only those things they find comfortable. All of teaching is about stretching students past their comfort levels. No more deference should be paid to the discomfort of public speaking than we pay to the discomfort of other subject matter. And remember, the discomfort goes away with experience.

How do I use such a complex rubric for a speaking activity?
Remember when I referred to the multiple-trait writing rubric? I had a writing rubric that had a category for content, word choice, voice, organization, sentence structure, and writing mechanics. (The writing mechanics category included punctuation, capitalization, and paragraphing, which seem like disparate items to me, so I might have preferred an even more complex rubric.) Giving six grades is certainly less convenient than giving one grade, but it is necessary.

Now, it seems, we have to make an eleven-trait speaking rubric, right? It may seem unwieldy, but you need to make it, nonetheless.

You don't need to use the entire rubric each time. Did I grade every writing assignment with the six-trait rubric? No. I had focus points. I might say, "Today as you respond to this prompt, focus on organization. I will not be looking for word choice or voice." Or I might say, "This time, make sure you add details to your writing, and let's concentrate on content." I only pulled out the entire rubric for the research paper.

Similarly, you should focus on particular skills for most class speaking assignments. In the current events discussion, grade content and poise one week, and grade content and voice the next week. For the book report, tell students they will be graded on content, organization, poise, and life. Bring out the entire rubric for the one major speaking assignment of the year.

I believe you will find it easier than you think to score PVLEGS as the students speak. You will become adept at recognizing the elements, and marking 4, 3, 2, 3, 3, 3 doesn't take much time. It is harder to listen for all the elements of building a speech as the words are flying by. Did she include all of the requirements? Were there significant signposts? How many connectors were there? A solution may be to have the script in front of you. You required that the student write it, and you insist that it can't be used during the speech, so collect it and refer to it to make sure you didn't miss anything.

A major speech assignment takes a lot of time. Thirty students times five minutes a speech? What teacher can afford that time commitment?
It is worse than you think. Five minutes of talking time, plus the two minutes it takes for the class to score the speech, plus three minutes for one student to sit down and the next to get ready. So thirty students times *ten* minutes a speech is more realistic. Three hundred minutes. Five hours. An entire week of language arts class or social studies out the window. Many teachers will have already given up time for student presentations, of course, and for them, only a little extra time is involved for student scoring. Still, it is undeniable that speaking activities take time. You could cover a lot of material with those five hours if you lectured instead. You could hand out a lot of test preparation worksheets. There are a couple of ways to address this question.

First, let me reiterate the goal here: to prepare students for life. Aren't speaking skills worth one week of the thirty-six or so weeks in the school year? Second, the time is not wasted. Students listening to presentations are learning about the planets or environmental issues or biomes or Supreme Court cases from the speeches. It is not as if there is no content being presented. Students presenting are probably getting a deeper understanding of their topic than they would get from reading the textbook. There is still subject matter learning going on, in addition to the valuable practice for a life of oral communication.

Finally, teachers are pack rats. I had this demonstrated by Mary, a team-mate who retired in 2004. When she retired, she put out all of the materials she would no longer be using and offered them to all of us for use in our classes. It was an amazing pile of stuff. She had workbooks with handouts that had to be run on a mimeograph machine. Most of the readers of this book probably don't know what a mimeograph machine is. She had materials three decades old. Mary is not unique. Many teachers have all kinds of old items that they are reluctant to throw away.

What does this have to do with the time issue? Most teachers have pack rat tendencies in their curriculum, too. I got tired of people coming to workshops and saying, "I know you have a lot on your plates, but here is the new thing you should teach." What they should have said is, "Some of the stuff on your plate has to be scraped off and discarded." I guarantee you that you have some old unit you have been teaching for years that can go away. (If you are new to the profession, you were probably given some things to teach that have *always* been taught in the school.)

When I moved to civics from English, I was told that they always taught about the Articles of Confederation for two weeks before they taught about the Constitution. How often have the Articles of Confederation come up in your life so far? If they ever come up, Google them. I never taught the Articles of Confederation. I had two extra weeks to play with, and not one person ever came to me upset about my decision. You have something that can go. It hurts to say that, but it's true. Something can be cut to make room for something new and more important and more relevant.

REFERENCES

Adams, Raymond S., and Bruce Jesse Biddle. 1970. *Realities of Teaching: Explorations with Video Tape.* New York: Holt, Rinehart and Winston.

Kinsella, W. P. 1982. *Shoeless Joe.* New York: Ballantine.

Merriam-Webster. 1998. *Collegiate Dictionary.* 10th ed. Springfield, MA: Merriam-Webster.

National Association of Colleges and Employers. 2010. "Top Skills for Job Candidates." *Job Outlook 2011.* http://naceweb.org/Press/Releases/Top_Skills_for_Job_Candidates.aspx?referal=pressroom&menuid=273.

Stevens, Betsy. 2005. "What Communication Skills Do Employers Want? Silicon Valley Recruiters Respond." *Journal of Employment Counseling* 42: 2–9.

Witt, Christopher. 2009. *Real Leaders Don't Do PowerPoint.* New York: Crown Business.